SILENT Eviᴅᴇɴᴄᴇ

Inside the Police Search for
Ben and Olivia

SILENT EVIDENCE

Inside the Police Search for Ben and Olivia

John Goulter

RANDOM HOUSE
NEW ZEALAND

A RANDOM HOUSE BOOK
Published by
Random House New Zealand
18 Poland Road, Glenfield, Auckland, New Zealand

First published 2000
© 2000 John Goulter

ISBN 1 86941 386 5

Photograph credits: NZ Police
Printed by Publishing Press Ltd, Auckland

CONTENTS

THANKS AND EXPLANATIONS

It is impossible to thank sufficiently the families of Olivia Hope and Ben Smart for their help. At the outset, Gerald and Jan Hope and John and Mary Smart each had differing attitudes to the writing of a book. Their feelings ranged from trust and hope that the project would be worthy of the experience, to strong misgivings. I told them I hoped the book would stand as a tribute and a memorial to their lost children. I hope that more strongly now I know a bit more of the ordeal the two families went through. Thank you.

I owe a huge acknowledgement to Rob Pope and his team. Once Rob decided to help me with the book, he and other members of Operation Tam gave a lot of their time, memories and insights. I think they hoped that a story that had already been 'told' to a greater extent than virtually any other New Zealand crime would at last be told fully. There was a desire among some in the police team to set the record straight. But I told Rob at the beginning that I wasn't setting out merely to tell the police side of a story that had generated a lot of heat and criticism. He said he expected 'warts and all' and asked only that I be fair.

In the course of writing the book, I talked to many people, both inside the police and elsewhere, who expected that I would have an 'agenda': to prove Scott Watson's guilt, or argue for his innocence; to show that the police were on the right track all along, or expose a bungled investigation; to reveal how the media had jeopardised a massively complex investigation by trying to second-guess the police at every turn, or how shamelessly they had exploited two grieving families to sell newspapers and push up their ratings. I tried to explain that I wouldn't be trying to relitigate thousands of hours of inquiry, analysis and legal arguments. I said I would be setting out to recount what happened, because that was what the story deserved.

For what it is worth, I now think that despite problems, a few misjudgements and many tensions along the way, Operation Tam was conducted comprehensively and skilfully, sometimes even heroically. I was impressed by how deeply the members of Operation Tam cared about what they were doing, and how professionally they did it most of the time.

I think that while police sometimes believed many of the media were shallow, sensational and even dangerous in their reporting of the disappearances, the investigation and the trial, most of the reporting was fair and humane. No matter how much they wanted a story, most of the reporters were, in the end, much like the rest of us: sad and angry that such an awful thing had happened and concerned about the grief-stricken families at the centre of it.

I think that members of Ben's and Olivia's families have been truly courageous in the way they have coped with a terrible plight with patience and dignity.

Many other people in Marlborough and elsewhere gave me a lot of their time and recollections. Most are named in the text. Some, for legal and other reasons, are not. I am grateful to them all.

I owe much more than the normal thanks to the people who helped with the production of the book. Jenny Hellen, at Random House, was both persistent and patient with a project that had more than its share of difficulties. Jane Parkin, of

Wellington, took on a bigger responsibility than I think book editors usually have to shoulder. She was encouraging and professional throughout. I claim the errors and omissions as my own; the order and consistency are Jane's, and the credit for finishing the project at all is Jenny's.

I am very thankful to Juliet Ashton who attended much of the trial at the High Court in Wellington when I was busy over the road. My son Robbie also helped keep the clippings file in order.

The place over the road where I was busy was the office of Jenny Shipley. She and her staff understood when I occasionally had to disappear from the office to catch up with the book. Like most New Zealanders, Jenny Shipley had a strong concern with the case and, like a staggering number of other people, some personal connections that made it very real for her.

When I took the job in the Prime Minister's Office, I worried I would be compromised in writing the book. And it was odd juggling issues such as the storm over INCIS, allegations of police under-funding and the fallout from police restructuring and then going home to write about people at the sharp end of it, including a detective inspector who was worried about whether his job would survive the restructuring.

And there were times when the two roles looked like getting confused. The Scott Watson guilty verdict came through in the thick of the APEC leaders' meeting in Auckland. When Jenny Shipley asked me to get the families on the phone so she could pass on her hope that they might at last be feeling some relief, it was hard to remember whether I was working on the book or serving the Prime Minister.

I suppose that the story of Ben and Olivia that touched so many people who shared the same outrage and sorrow reminded us what a small country New Zealand still is, in ways we are all thankful for.

FOREWORD

I never met Olivia Hope or Ben Smart. Nor did anyone else in the investigation team. But over the course of Operation Tam, we all felt we got to know them a little even though it can sometimes be easy to overlook the victims of crime within the hurried activity of an investigation. This book, *Silent Evidence*, is not about the courts, crown, police or defence. In many respects it is about a community and its collective response to a terrible murder.

But more than that, *Silent Evidence* stands as a tribute to two people who encapsulate the spirit of Marlborough youth: their vibrant personalities, their talents, the values they represented and their aspirations, which will never be realised. This is a book about Ben and Olivia.

Inevitably the police investigation forms an integral part of the telling of this story, but it can never be a complete story. It would be impossible to draw together a comprehensive picture from the hundreds of thousands of police and court documents that have been compiled.

While the police have supplied information to ensure reasonable accuracy, the contents of *Silent Evidence* do not reflect the police position. Where police officers have been interviewed, their personal comments, opinions and recollections, are exactly that, no more.

There may be a public perception that homicide inquiries are exciting, action-packed affairs. In reality, investigations are tedious and laborious, requiring significant personal and group discipline over extended periods. There are no flashes of investigative brilliance. It is plain hard work.

Criminal inquiries deal with a certain sad element of human behaviour and all its associated frailties. Commonly held concepts of morality and rationality do not seem to exist in the minds of offenders. Criminals regularly distance themselves from crimes; they do not just give themselves up. Against such a background, absolute answers rarely exist. It is not always possible to put every piece back in the jigsaw – that is the nature of both crime and life. *Silent Evidence* provides an insight into the challenges and demands faced by the dedicated group of men and women who formed the Operation Tam team, of which I was privileged to be a part.

For various reasons this case has received a high level of media and public attention, with considerable debate arising from that. Media reports, by their very nature, can often generalise issues and in the process ignore important detail. I would hope that *Silent Evidence*'s examination of the facts will help people to form more balanced and informed viewpoints.

The public and private tragedy of Olivia's and Ben's deaths will always remain with Jan, Gerald, Mary, John and their families. The personal and community grieving will continue. If *Silent Evidence* serves as a form of memorial to a daughter and son who will never experience the opportunity of a full life, then it has achieved its purpose.

Detective Inspector Rob Pope
New Zealand Police

I

THE SCENE

WHEN THE SUN ROSE OVER the sleeping bays and inlets of the Marlborough Sounds on New Year's Day 1998 it was the beginning of yet another perfect El Niño summer day. If any were awake to see the early light, they would have seen all about them the beauty that makes the Sounds a summertime playground, a piece of paradise that matches the promise of Marlborough's tourist brochures: *Discover Paradise*.

The dawn of 1 January 1998 held a particular interest for one group in Marlborough. They saw the sunrise from the summit of the region's highest peak, Mt Tapuae-o-Uenuku, in an attempt to establish if it might be the first piece of mainland New Zealand to see the light of a new year. In two years' time it would be a nice fillip for Marlborough if the province could claim to be the first in the country – and so the world – to be touched by the light of a new millennium.

In its way, that exercise was right for the 'new' Marlborough. Once it was a sleepy province, a place people passed through after a Cook Strait crossing, or visited to spend long summer weeks in isolated baches, or boating and fishing. Wellington may be just across the water, and Christchurch a few hours down the beautiful Kaikoura coast road, but the Sounds could be in a different, untouched world. But now the region was changing, and its wineries, olive groves and mussel farms were helping to seal Marlborough's reputation as a trend-setter for the new millennium – though the climbers just missed out on making that point. They recorded sunrise on Tapuae-o-Uenuku at 5.41 a.m., but Mt Hikurangi, near Gisborne, beat Marlborough's mountain by 45 seconds.

So Marlborough would escape the hordes and hangers-on that a big millennium celebration would bring. Maybe it was just as well. Today, locals had their own celebrations to recover from. The Sounds had seen in the New Year in all the traditional places, the way it had for years. In outposts like the Portage, and Furneaux Lodge in Endeavour Inlet, parties had pumped *Auld Lang Syne* and Blur's *Song 2* – with its yell-along 'wooo-hooo!' chorus, it was the big party song that summer – virtually until the dawn. These rowdy celebrations have long been a ritual in the Sounds, bringing together an extraordinary mix: kids fresh out of the local colleges, Marlborough Boys' and Marlborough Girls'; wandering backpackers; bach-owners on their big annual holiday; passing fishermen who know where to throw anchor and get a night to remember; alternative lifestylers down from their blocks of marginal land around the Sounds; a lot of desperate-to-party regulars from the Picton pubs; and a few itinerants whom nobody can rightly place.

The best way to do it, if you have the right friends or can raise the money, is to get a group together, charter a yacht and head out to a destination such as Furneaux for the big bash. Afterwards, you can sleep off the party on the boat and make your way back to Picton over the next day or two. Second best, you can catch a water taxi from Picton to Furneaux, have a good blow-out, and get the water taxi back. Operators such as the Cougar Line put on extra boats to deal with the party crowd.

This year all had apparently gone well. Constable Mike Porter, of Picton, told the *Marlborough Express* that police were pleased with the way revellers had welcomed in the year.

Alongside its photo of Marlborough's first baby of the year, the *Express* devoted its first lead story of 1998 to the party-goers' good behaviour. Porter said the crowd on the Picton foreshore peaked between 1 a.m. and 3 a.m. when the boatloads returned from Furneaux. They had been in a 'happy' mood, and few problems had been encountered.

But of course the Furneaux Lodge party had ended far from happily – though maybe only one of the hundreds of party-goers who had been there and were now sleeping off the celebrations knew anything about that. Within days, the entire nation would be hungry for information about precisely what had happened to two young people from the party. Porter himself would spend most of the coming year trying to map, down to the last minute, everything that had happened at Furneaux Lodge throughout the evening and early morning. The party was transformed into a sort of virtual event, analysed from every possible angle to try to construct a picture of the last minutes of the lives of Ben Smart and Olivia Hope. And although it took months, and never produced a definitive picture, very soon all the computing power and analysis, and thousands of hours and millions of dollars' worth of searching and detective work, came to focus on a few minutes around that instant that had already made the headlines. At 5.41 a.m., when the sun of the New Year first touched the summit of Mt Tapuae-o-Uenuku, something terrible, apparently, was happening to Ben and Olivia.

Ben Smart and Olivia Hope had, separately, set out for the New Year's party 'down in the Sounds', as locals say, just a day or two earlier. Ben was heading for a bach in Camp Bay near Punga Cove, just around Endeavour Inlet from Furneaux Lodge. He had originally planned to sail down on one of the yachts heading for the inlet, but when he found there wasn't enough room he decided to drive to Punga Cove in his blue

Mini with a mate, Gareth Vincent. The narrow, largely unsealed road from Linkwater along Kenepuru Road and up Titirangi Road over the Kenepuru Saddle to Punga Cove is the only road access to Endeavour Inlet. From Punga Cove, the only way to Furneaux Lodge is by boat or a solid walk along the section of the Queen Charlotte Walkway that hugs the shore of Big Bay and then runs all the way to the top of the inlet. A bunch of guys were planning to spend New Year at the bach, hanging out during the day and heading over to Furneaux Lodge for the big night. Ben left home at about midday on Monday 29 December, telling his parents, John and Mary, that he'd be back by the following Saturday or Sunday.

Before he left for work that Monday, John had something of a warning for his son, but it had nothing to do with the perils of a rowdy New Year's party. 'I remember talking to him and saying, "Be careful of the road",' John Smart recalled months later with a shrug and a sad stare into the middle distance. 'I told him it was a narrow, winding road with a lot of logging trucks. But that was the only warning I gave him. I thought it was a good place to go for a New Year's Eve celebration, a pretty safe place.'

Ben was 21, after all, and after boarding school and then flatting in Christchurch, he was used to looking after himself. He planned to return to his parents' home in central Blenheim in time to start back at work at his father's engineering firm on Monday 5 January. 'We didn't say, "When are you going to be home?"' Mary said. 'He had been living on his own for three years in Christchurch. And he just said, "I'll be back before Monday. I might come back Friday, I don't know, it might be Saturday." So it was okay, we'll see you when we see you.'

Olivia Hope left for Furneaux on Tuesday 30 December after a day's work at the Wairau River winery where she was earning money waitressing before her first year at university in 1998. With her older sister, 19-year-old Amelia, she would join up with a group of young people who had chartered a yacht, the *Tamarack*, to sail down to Furneaux. She packed her gear before leaving for work at the winery and, straight after work, left the family home in Grovetown, just out of Blenheim, to drive with Amelia to Whatamango Bay to join the *Tamarack*.

'She was really excited about it,' her mother, Jan, later told police. 'She seemed almost more excited about going out on the boat than New Year's Eve.' Olivia's father, Gerald, also noticed how excited she was about the trip. 'She had been talking about it for days.'

Gerald and Jan regarded Olivia as mature for 17, but Gerald, who was at home when Olivia left, had some parental advice for her. It was mainly about water safety, being careful getting on and off the yacht into a dinghy or Naiad to go ashore. He was worried that Olivia was not a strong swimmer, and with her slim build she would not last long in the water if she fell in. Although she had spent time in the Sounds and was familiar with the family's runabout, Olivia had had no experience with yachts and was no sailor. 'I also spoke to her about alcohol and being in control of herself. I emphasised if she was going ashore she had to eat before she went to the New Year's party, and she took food for that.' Olivia's response to the parting lecture would be familiar to any parent of a teenager: 'Trust me, Dad. I'm big enough, I'm going to university next year.'

Until their last minutes, the days that Ben and Olivia spent in the Sounds were almost entirely unexceptional – the sort of summer break that thousands of young kids enjoy for New Year. After Christmas with the family, New Year is for friends. Some parents might be surprised at the amount of drinking that went on, along with a bit of dope smoking. But a dissection of their own teenagers' parties would probably turn up a similar picture. Olivia herself packed four small bottles of Montana Brightstone cider, a bottle of Lindauer Brut and a hip flask of Jim Beam bourbon along with three days' supply of food as her and her sister Amelia's contribution to the *Tamarack*'s supplies. From the start, the tragedy of Ben and Olivia was written up as the end of innocence in the Sounds, 'death in paradise', or some such variation; but this was paradise on a big night out, a long way from the parents.

There were 10 or 11 people on board the chartered *Tamarack* for Olivia's trip to Furneaux. They were mainly friends of Amelia, who was already studying at Otago University, but Olivia was accustomed to hanging out with that crowd.

For their first night out, the *Tamarack* moored at a bay near Kumutoto in the Sounds. At about 7.30 a.m., Olivia phoned home to tell her mother that everything was fine; they were having a good time and she was about to have a swim. Jan warned Olivia that she had a really long day ahead, and not to push it. Later that day, New Year's Eve, the *Tamarack* sailed back to Picton to pick up a couple more who had booked for the trip. Then mid-afternoon the group set sail directly for Furneaux. Most of the group began drinking during the two- to three-hour trip, and there was only one 'incident' along the way. It was about a night out in Christchurch a couple of months earlier, when Olivia had wanted to leave the group she was with to go off with a guy she had met. This had apparently annoyed her friend Anna Cunliffe, who had been left with people she hardly knew. Now, going over the incident with Anna on the *Tamarack*, Olivia became upset, mainly because she thought her friend still bore a grudge. After some consoling from friends, Olivia wiped away her tears and the incident blew over.

Almost immediately after arriving at Endeavour Inlet in the early evening, the group changed and went ashore to Furneaux Lodge, using either the Naiad water taxis that the Lodge put on for the benefit of patrons, or a speedboat that belonged to a friend, Duncan Anderson. Recollections of the evening are, inevitably, hazy, confused and often conflicting, but what follows of Olivia and Ben's movements are the facts that are not disputed.

The party at Furneaux was hardly getting going when the *Tamarack* group arrived, but the management had made plans for what, on past experience, could turn out to be a fairly wild night. Olivia's bourbon was confiscated, and the Lodge and its grounds were declared a no-glass area. All drinks consumed that evening had to be bought on the premises, and were served in plastic. Early on Olivia met up with friends, mainly seventh formers from Marlborough Girls' College, and for the rest of the evening her sister, Amelia, saw little of her. The scene at Furneaux had two main focuses – the bar in the Lodge itself, and the outdoor garden bar and linked dance floor down nearer the foreshore. The young crowd, including Olivia and her friends, spent most of their time down there, visiting the Lodge only occasionally to buy a drink from the bar or use the Eftpos machine in the office, across the hall from the bar.

Sometime in the early evening, Olivia's image was captured on videotape. Kenneth Spicer was an English tourist recording his New Zealand holiday. At about 8.30 p.m. he panned his camera around the lawn in front of the Lodge, and the picture he recorded shows Olivia with a group of young people on the corner of the veranda, outside the main bar. In the video, Olivia is clearly wearing a black top and black jeans, and her hair is not tied back. Ben is less easy to see, but is wearing one of his personal trademarks – a backwards baseball cap.

For much of the evening, from about 7.30 p.m. until at least 11 p.m., Olivia was with Hamish Rose. The 21-year-old was a good friend of the Hope family; his father owned the Wairau River vineyard where Jan Hope was a manager and where Olivia had been doing holiday work. He was staying in a tent at the Lodge's campsite, where a lot of the out-of-towners, including a group of girls from Rangi Ruru Girls' School in Christchurch, camped for the party. He had taken a walk around the Lodge grounds and was on his way to the campsite when he ran into Olivia with a couple of other girls. Olivia told him she was 'pretty pissed', but to Hamish she didn't show it. Initially, Olivia and Hamish went back to his tent where she had a beer and they talked with the people at the campsite. Olivia didn't know any of them well, so after about half an hour she suggested to Hamish that they go to the Lodge, where he bought them drinks from the bar – a beer for himself and a bourbon for Olivia. They took their drinks outside to drink on the lawn, and after a few minutes Olivia suggested going down to the jetty to try to get back her confiscated flask of bourbon. She pointed out the man who had taken it and Hamish asked him about the chances of getting it back. He said it might be possible, but not to count on it.

They sat on the lawn and chatted for half an hour or so, then walked back up to the Lodge where they ran into a couple of Olivia's friends. When Hamish said he was going back to the campsite to change out of his shorts, Olivia told him to make sure he came back, and she gave him her watch to make sure he did. He thought it was 'a little unusual' that Olivia wanted to spend so much time with him – and his mates back at the tent were pissed off that he had broken from the crowd to spend time with a girl – but he wasn't bothered by it. He had a beer with the boys before returning to the Lodge, where he found Olivia outside, much where he had left her. They went inside and bought more drinks. Outside again, Olivia suggested they go for a walk, so they wandered down to the jetty and sat on a seat overlooking the beach. They talked, kissed, and walked back up to the garden bar. It was well dark by now, and Olivia was getting cold. Hamish offered her his jersey but she didn't want to wear it. Pretty soon, Hamish saw some of his mates in the garden bar and said he was going off to have a drink with them. Olivia didn't want to go, and said she would look for her friends. That was the last Hamish saw of Olivia. But before he went, perhaps because he wasn't keen to leave a young girl by herself, he said to Olivia that he thought a friend of hers was around the Lodge somewhere. He knew they 'had had something going in the past'. They had a look for him but couldn't find him. His name was Ben Smart.

Ben had been among the first of the group to arrive at the Vercoe family bach at Punga Cove. Since arriving late on Monday 29 December, he and the growing bunch of guys – mainly old Marlborough Boys' and Christ's College friends – had sat around doing nothing much in particular. A lot of the time, Ben played his guitar, and there was a lot of drinking. At least some of the group smoked a few joints. It was definitely a 'boys at the bach' scene. The beers started with breakfast on New Year's Eve, and later the guys moved on to spirits. In the late afternoon they started to get ready for the Furneaux Lodge party, a short boat ride around the inner Endeavour Inlet. Ben got a ride to Furneaux at about 8 p.m. in a boat with Marko Doblanovic, one of the bach crowd. On the way, the early drinking took its toll and Ben threw up over the side of the boat.

Almost immediately after arriving at Furneaux, Ben visited the office to use the Eftpos machine to withdraw some money. Soon afterwards, he met his older sister, Rebecca. She had come over to the Lodge for the evening with a couple of Wellington friends on the Cougar Line ferry from the Portage, where she was staying. She had expected to come across her little brother that night; if she had thought about it, she'd probably also expected that he'd have a few drinks. He was known to like a beer, and to get very jolly with it. Tonight, he was on the lawn in front of the Lodge with Gareth Vincent, the mate who'd come up from Blenheim in his car. Rebecca could see that Ben was not exactly sober; he was very merry, laughing and joking a lot. He told Rebecca about having a spew on the boat but said he felt better after it. She told her little brother to slow down a bit. At 23, Rebecca was a couple of years older than Ben, but her concern was nothing more than any older sister's. The family knew he could handle himself.

Ben moved around during the evening, spending time with friends as he met them. One of them was his old girlfriend, Sally Ingram. They had gone out for about eight months before breaking up in November, but they remained good friends. Sally saw him first when he was getting some money. They met up two or three more times during the evening, generally outside near the garden bar, and had a couple of good talks. Sally could see he'd been drinking, but thought he seemed okay for it. As late as 11.15 p.m. she noticed that he was not slurring his words or anything. They spent time together then, and talked a lot about their relationship and how they were pleased to be good friends now. Just before midnight they said goodbye and went their separate ways.

But about half an hour later they ran into each other again, only long enough to wish each other a happy New Year. This time, Sally thought Ben appeared the worse for wear; he looked more drunk than he had earlier and was searching for his lighter. They had a conversation about what he was smoking. Ben said it was 'a special one', but Sally wasn't sure if it was dope, because the cigarette didn't look as if it had been rolled. A little later Sally caught sight of Ben again, in the distance by the tennis courts. He seemed to be with a girl.

It was around this time, about 12.30 a.m., that Ben ran into his sister Rebecca again. He introduced Rebecca to the girl he was with, but Rebecca didn't catch the name. The girl had long blonde hair, pulled or tied back; later, shown photographs, Rebecca agreed this was probably Olivia Hope. But her first acquaintance with Olivia – if it was her – was also the last time she saw Ben. Rebecca had a Cougar Line water taxi to catch at 1 a.m.

Many of the party-goers were leaving now, some back to their boats moored in the inlet, some to their baches in other parts of the Sounds, and some back on the boats to Picton. The mood of the evening changed with their departure. From now on there was less casual milling around and less dancing. The band packed up at about 1.30 a.m. – in fact the band's amplifiers had developed a fatal problem about two hours earlier, but they had kept the music coming with a DJ system, playing tapes and CDs, until deciding to call it a night. From now on, there was more serious drinking, in both the main bar and garden bar, and there were some increasingly serious brawls which security guards were called to break up.

The most objectively documented 'sighting' of Ben was at one minute past midnight. For his first act of the New Year, he went up to the office for another Eftpos transaction to withdraw some cash. By about 1 a.m. Ben and Olivia had got together and were seen with each other at various places around the Lodge – on the dance floor, in the garden bar, near the main bar. Some later said that Ben was looking visibly drunk by this time, but most of the observers were too.

At around 2 a.m. Kirsty Sutherland, a friend from school and one of the *Tamarack* crowd, came across Ben and Olivia, and suggested they pack it in. She was planning to head back to Punga Cove with some of the guys, and she convinced Ben and Olivia to come with her. The plan was to get a ride with Marko Doblanovic to the *Tamarack*. There the girls could get their gear for the night, and Marko would come back and pick them up. 'Ben had had a bit to drink and was sleepy,' Kirsty recalls. 'Olivia seemed all right. She had a bit to drink as well, and was just like ready to find a bed for the both of them.'

They got the ride to the *Tamarack* and gathered their gear together, but after a long wait on deck it became clear Marko wasn't coming back. They threw life jackets around their shoulders to keep warm, and Olivia became annoyed that heaps of people who hadn't paid were sleeping on the boat while she, who had contributed to the charter, couldn't get a bed. Ben was happy enough, though, dozing while the two girls talked, and occasionally laughing if something they said amused him.

At about 4 a.m. Amelia Hope and a friend, Rick Goddard, caught a Naiad water taxi out to the crowded *Tamarack*. Rick was one of the crowd staying with Ben at the Punga Cove bach, but he'd been unable to find a ride back and hoped that if he went to the *Tamarack* he could get a ride the rest of the way, maybe on Duncan Anderson's speedboat. The driver of the yellow Naiad was Guy Wallace, and as well as Amelia and Rick Goddard there were three other passengers: a couple who wanted to be taken to the Solitude Jetty, just around the inlet from Furneaux, and a man who was by himself. Amelia thought him fairly nondescript: white, reasonably short, with a medium build, and dark brown hair cut in a sort of crew cut. She reckoned he was about 25-plus.

The *Tamarack* was the Naiad's first port of call. As soon as they arrived, Amelia heard Olivia on deck saying there was no room and suggesting, apparently to Ben, that they catch the Naiad back to shore. She tried to get aboard but the water taxi driver stopped her, so she offered to pay if that was necessary. No, the driver explained, it was simply a case of displacement; to avoid excess weight in the little inflatable, she would have to wait until the *Tamarack* passengers got off before she and Ben got on.

Once it was safe to do so, she and Ben hopped on, Olivia carrying a red 'K2' backpack containing some clothes and, Kirsty thought, perhaps a brown sleeping bag. Kirsty had intended catching a ride on the Naiad as well, but in the end she missed the boat. She decided at the last minute not to take her pack with her, and while she was putting it away the Naiad left. Olivia called out, 'Where's Kirsty?' But Kirsty waved them off, saying to go ahead without her. She took no notice of where the Naiad headed with Ben and Olivia. Amelia Hope watched for an instant as the Naiad went past another yacht, the *Benedictine*. 'I recognised that yacht because some of my friends were on there. The Naiad looked like it was curving around the back of it. I didn't see where it went after that.'

The other couple on the inflatable were Sarah Dyer and Hayden Morrisey, but they have only hazy recollections of what happened next. Like most people at Furneaux, they had been drinking for much of the night. Sarah Dyer in fact thought the original couple on the Naiad, Amelia Hope and Rick Goddard, had stopped briefly at the *Tamarack* and got back onto the Naiad after learning their yacht was full. It was an easy mistake to make at about 4 a.m.; the Hope sisters, after all, looked reasonably alike.

But Guy Wallace, the taxi driver, had very firm memories of the short trip. He was working at Furneaux for a short term and was not, in fact, on water duty at all that night. He had been working in the bar during the busiest hours, and at about 4 a.m., with customers dwindling, he had left to take a break and begin the big clear-up job around the Lodge grounds. It was only when he came across a few groups desperate for taxi rides – most of them had been turned down by the regular drivers who were now off duty – that he decided to do a few runs in the Naiad. He did about four trips, one of which brought together the couple who wanted to go to the *Tamarack* with the lone man wanting to get to his boat and the couple who wanted to get to Solitude Jetty. While dropping off Amelia Hope and Rick Goddard at the *Tamarack*, he had a conversation with the girl he subsequently found to be Olivia, who offered to pay for a ride. He told her and the guy with her that wouldn't be necessary, but to wait until the others had got off the Naiad. He believed Olivia wasn't carrying a sleeping bag, just a handbag. Getting on the Naiad, she called out to a girl on the *Tamarack*, asking if she wanted to come too, but the girl decided to stay. According to the people on board the *Tamarack*, the time was about 4 a.m. or 4.20 a.m.

On the Naiad, Olivia complained that though she had paid to sleep on the *Tamarack*, there was no room. Her male friend, whom Guy Wallace later learned was Ben, thanked him for letting them on the boat but didn't say much. Guy said the two of them had been drinking, but didn't seem too bad. Wallace told Olivia to sit beside the lone man, to keep the boat balanced; then, once they were under way, Olivia asked Wallace if he knew of anywhere to stay. The lone man piped up and said, 'You can stay on my boat, but he can't.' At the time, Wallace thought it was just a throwaway line, made without any malice. The stranger then pointed out the direction of the boat he was heading for. Wallace got the instruction, but didn't remember the name of the boat.

As the Naiad approached this boat, rafted up with a group of what Wallace believed to be four or five others, Ben joked to the stranger: 'Please tell me that's it,' and pointed to a big Markline.

'No, but it's tied next to it if that helps,' the stranger said.

'No worries,' Ben said. 'That's cool.'

When they reached the man's boat, Olivia was first off the Naiad, followed by Ben. 'This is really nice of you,' Olivia said. 'Are you sure there's enough room?'

The stranger replied that there was heaps.

Wallace then had what he later described as momentary misgivings about dropping off the young couple, and asked Ben and Olivia if they were okay with the arrangement. They said it was fine. Everyone exchanged New Year's wishes and Wallace headed off. He noticed that the boat was an old but very well-maintained timber ketch – a two-masted vessel which was pretty unusual around the Sounds. He said it was white with a dark blue strip above the waterline, and he noticed a lot of roping on board.

Guy Wallace later offered a remarkably good description of the man. He assessed him as about 32 years old, 5'8" (170 cm) tall, of a wiry build, with a couple of days' growth on his face, and brownish wavy hair. He was wearing a short-sleeved Levi shirt of a khaki to pale-green colour, with jeans and, probably, sandshoes. He looked 'bourboned up, like his eyes weren't focusing'.

Wallace watched the three of them as they got onto the man's boat, but he didn't see them go below deck. That was the last anybody saw of Ben or Olivia.

Or the last reliable sighting. Much later, Robert Mullin, who worked at Furneaux and drove one of the water taxis, reckoned he saw Ben and another guy on the jetty at Furneaux, looking down at the fish. But that sighting, just before dawn on New Year's Day, was discredited as yet another piece of information from a witness who'd had too much to drink, no watch on his wrist and a poor grasp of time.

In the coming months, so much of what happened at Furneaux during that night when 1997 ticked over to 1998 was to become foggy and disputed. Ask any person what they did at a big and rowdy New Year party and the answer is likely to be hazy. Ask several hundred, and confusion, mistimed sightings and contradictions are inevitable. The picture fractures into a hundred different memories. Yet within a couple of days, police would have to start trying to assemble the night into a story that made sense and explained what had happened to Ben and Olivia. As they did so, some pictures, like Ben down at the jetty staring at the fish, like Guy Wallace's recollections of the boat he delivered the couple to, would have to be discounted as merely wrong and unreliable.

But for a minute it is tempting to hold on to that picture of Ben down at the pre-dawn jetty as an alternative ending to the Furneaux party – the version that should have happened. He would find somewhere to lie down, sleep off the big night, and tomorrow or the next day, or the day after that, he'd throw his guitar back in the blue Mini and head home. In his bedroom he would put on one of his CDs. For the sake of our alternative story, it would be U2. Rock neanderthals, maybe, but he liked them a lot. He would perhaps recall the day in Christchurch when he had gone out to the airport to see the band arrive in the city. He had scored a souvenir photograph of himself with U2's guitarist, The Edge. With his own band, Exit, Ben was making some good cash and entertaining ideas of making it big. But dreams are easy when you're 21. In the real world he was buckling down to some serious work in his father's engineering firm and proving that, after a year or two of marking time, he had what it takes to make a good career in that line of work.

Still, wind up the stereo a bit louder and let U2 belt out 'New Year's Day'. It had to be one of their best anthems. The lyrics said that nothing much changes on New Year's Day. And nothing much would have changed for Ben and Olivia if New Year's Eve had been the happy event that had been reported at the time.

2

MISSING PERSONS

Aの L THOUGH THE DISAPPEARANCE of Ben and Olivia was about to become the biggest story in New Zealand in 1998, for the first day and a half of the year the Sounds kept their secret. Among the *Tamarack* crowd on New Year's morning, the first reaction to Olivia's disappearance was irritation. Kirsty Sutherland and some others had set out to shore about 9 a.m. to see where she had ended up sleeping. They couldn't find her anywhere, and after about an hour of asking around, became annoyed. It was, after all, not unheard of for Olivia to go off without the crowd; she had done it in Christchurch a couple of months earlier. Nor was it particularly worrying. Amelia Hope knew that some of Olivia's friends had tents in the Furneaux campsite, so she could have gone there. It did not seem particularly unusual, either, for Olivia to have gone off with Ben. Although they were only friends, they had got together a few other times for what a friend of Olivia's later described as 'one-night stands'.

Kirsty Sutherland went to Hamish Rose's tent when she was looking for Olivia, but he knew nothing. 'I just assumed that she was somewhere with Ben,' Hamish recalled. 'I wasn't really concerned at that point.' Ben was a responsible guy, he thought, but he was also pretty easy-going. It wouldn't worry him if he was a bit late getting home. Later that day, Hamish and his friends went out on the inlet for some water-skiing.

By about 10.30 a.m. Amelia Hope decided to head back to Picton because the chartered *Tamarack* was due back. On the way they stopped at Punga Cove, where they dropped off Kirsty Sutherland and asked a couple of the guys there if they had seen Ben or Olivia. They hadn't, but they didn't see any reason for concern. Ben was a sociable guy who liked a party, and it was just like him to change plans at the last minute, to go with the flow. The *Tamarack* headed back to Picton, stopping at Gem Resort on the way.

Gerald and Jan Hope's fears were first raised on mid-afternoon on New Year's Day. They were themselves out on the Sounds, spending several days with friends at Whatamango Bay, near Waikawa. They had spent New Year's Eve there and they spent the first day of the new year out on the water in the bay, swimming and water-skiing. In the middle of the afternoon on New Year's Day the *Tamarack* sailed into Whatamango Bay, as planned, to off-load some personal belongings and a few of the young people who were on board. Because the bay was quite shallow, with no jetty, the people and belongings were to be transferred ashore by the boat the Hopes were on.

Olivia was not on board, when the *Tamarack* met up with the Hopes' boat. When they asked Amelia where Olivia was, she said, "Oh, she has gone off with Ben. We couldn't find her." From that moment, Jan and Gerald Hope were both concerned. They were so worried, in fact, that they ended their boating holiday with their friends and, just after 6 p.m., went ashore and returned to their Grovetown home.

"That evening and night we waited for a phone call from Olivia," Gerald Hope said later. "In the morning after breakfast we decided to draw up a list of possible contacts, and set about ringing anyone who would have some knowledge as to where they were."

Jan was initially angry with Olivia when she had still not turned up at home by the morning of Friday 2 January. She was supposed to start work at the winery that day. Over the course of the Friday, she and Gerald became really worried. They made persistent calls to Furneaux Lodge and Punga Lodge and even offered money to people if they would check out the camping ground at Furneaux, and more particularly at Punga Lodge where Ben Smart was supposed to be staying.

They believed they were exhausting all the possible inquiries they could make on their own and decided early on that if by 3 p.m. they had turned up nothing, they would call the police. Becoming increasingly desperate, they arranged for several friends to travel to Endeavour Inlet to try to track down the water taxi driver who, they had established, had taken Ben and Olivia out to a boat. They called everyone they could think of including, of course, the Smarts.

Ben's mother, Mary Smart, recalls sitting in the sunny family room at the back of their beautifully restored Blenheim home when she received a worried, even angry call from Jan Hope. Jan's anxiety had clearly been brewing since Amelia had returned home the day before and told them about Olivia going missing. Her daughter had apparently last been seen jumping on a Naiad with Ben Smart.

'I'm really concerned, because Olivia was last seen with Ben jumping off the boat she had hired, and she was screaming and yelling because her friends had taken over the *Tamarack*,' Jan told Mary. 'She was last seen with Ben. Where is Ben?' she demanded.

Surprised at the emotional call, Mary told Jan she didn't know where Ben was, but he had been staying at Punga Cove and they weren't sure when he was coming back. It probably wouldn't be until Saturday or Sunday.

Mary's attitude didn't ease Jan's fears. 'I'll leave it another hour or so and if I haven't heard I'm going to ring the cops,' she said.

Mary got off the phone and remarked to her daughter Rebecca how uptight Jan seemed about the two kids.

'Well, I'm really worried too,' Rebecca told her mother.

Mary still believed the fears were groundless. 'I'm not a bit concerned,' she said. Rebecca was already acquainted with sudden loss of a very public sort. Joy Brander, the mother of her boyfriend, Jeremy, was one of those killed in the Raurimu massacre, in the central North Island, early in 1997. Rebecca had been going out with Jeremy for nearly six years, and she had worked for Joy Brander during university holidays, so she felt the loss keenly.

In fact Gerald and Jan Hope did not wait another hour or so before contacting the police. At 3.20 p.m. Gerald went down to the Blenheim Police Station and reported that his daughter hadn't been seen since about 4 a.m. the previous day. Constable Joe Kelly was the duty watch-house keeper, and he filled out a missing persons report and gave Gerald the usual advice: make some inquiries, call around anywhere she might be, such as at friends and relatives, and be patient. As it happened, Kelly knew Olivia. He had been the local youth education officer for Blenheim, and he had come across her through her activities with SADD, Students Against Drunk Driving.

But Gerald didn't feel his report had been taken seriously enough. He told John and Mary Smart the initial reaction had been, 'Like, yeah, yeah, yeah, we've got 10 other people whose kids haven't turned up.'

The Smarts, at least, thought that was an entirely understandable response; but Inspector Steve Caldwell, officer in charge of the Blenheim police, was still defensive months later about what he saw as suggestions that the inquiry took too long to get started. He defended the initial decision to keep cool. 'Now bearing in mind the time of the year, New Year's Eve, and the fact that we are dealing with two teenagers, the report was taken as a matter of routine,' Caldwell said. Police advice that the Hopes go away and make a few inquiries was nothing more or less than normal practice: 'Joe Kelly did the right thing.' Whether Gerald Hope thought the low-key response was the right one is another matter. But whatever the outcome, it was bound to be a sensitive case. Gerald Hope was a local councillor – he had unsuccessfully run for mayor last time around – and a prominent citizen who believed he had the ear of the media.

At 5 p.m. Gerald phoned the police back. He had made all the calls he could think of and drawn a blank. One of them was another call to the Smarts, and this time he had spoken with John. Gerald explained that Olivia was supposed to be back at work at the vineyard that morning and she would never have simply not turned up. For one thing, she was really excited about the job. The same message was brought home to the Smarts when a friend dropped around. She was a teacher at Marlborough Girls' College and she knew Olivia. She said Olivia would never, ever, fail to turn up for a job she was keen to have. She was such a reliable person.

By now, the Smart family, too, were becoming very concerned – not so much on Ben's account but because Olivia was missing and Ben seemed to be involved. 'That,' Mary recalled later, 'is when I said to John, "I'm not worried", and he said, "Well, I'm very worried." That was when it all started. From there on it was like being anaesthetised with shock for the next month.'

Gerald Hope's second call to the police did launch some serious attempts at investigation. Picton police were told about the situation, and photographs of Ben and Olivia were obtained from the families and faxed through to Furneaux Lodge. Rob Radcliffe, a detective at Picton, got on a boat and went down to Furneaux that evening to find out what he could. He was particularly interested in talking to the water taxi drivers, but he was exasperated to find that they seemed to have few precise recollections of trips they had done that night, and certainly none of Ben and Olivia's alleged last ride. John Mullen, whom Radcliffe took to be in charge of the water taxi drivers, could shed no light on what had happened. 'He wasn't particularly helpful because he couldn't remember,' Steve Caldwell recalls. 'I mean, there were thousands of people there, and he couldn't even remember when he knocked off.' To make matters worse, most of the water taxi drivers had had a few drinks after they finished work.

That night, at 9.25 p.m., Steve Caldwell was rung at home and told about the missing persons inquiry. He told staff to enter the details in the police computer system so other stations would know if they came across the kids in their own work. And he gave a direction for their banks to check their accounts for any transactions that might show where they had gone, or, if there had been foul play, if the culprit was using their bank cards.

Steve Caldwell is still on his guard about those early decisions. 'That's probably something that a lot of people don't realise, that we got on the case straight away, bearing in mind the bloody nonsense that was subsequently put into the media.' In a situation like that, police have to make a judgement call and, according to Caldwell, the early call, made within hours of learning Ben and Olivia were missing, was to escalate the inquiry far more quickly than would normally be the case when a couple of young people go missing after a party. And Gerald Hope's attitude had a lot to do with that decision.

'Obviously what we were picking up from Gerald was that it wasn't normal, it was out of character,' Caldwell says. 'In the normal set of circumstances, when you are dealing with teenagers who have gone missing for 24 hours, the alarm bells don't start ringing until people come to us and say, Look we have seen them get into a bloody car with a dodgy-looking character, or something like that. But we had none of that.

'But Gerald had already gone down the road that we would normally go down, saying, Look, they're at someone's place, they're being irresponsible, they will turn up. He had been through all that, and his body language or whatever, what he was saying, must have conveyed to Joe Kelly that this was out of character, that it couldn't be explained by normal circumstances.'

While police were getting to work with their inquiries, the Smarts had a barbecue to attend at the home of Mary's brother-in-law, Keith Reid. Rebecca decided to stay home in case there were any phone calls about Ben. At the barbecue, John and Keith agreed that the following morning they would travel down to Furneaux to see what they could find out. On the way back, John and Mary called in at the Hopes' Grovetown home to see if there was any news. They found Gerald and Jan beside themselves with worry. John asked Gerald if he wanted to join him and his brother-in-law on their trip to Furneaux the next morning. But Gerald said the police were arranging their own search party and, while they were taking a while to get organised, he would wait and go down with the main police party. John and Mary headed home, increasingly worried.

When they got there the nightmare seemed to be over. There was Ben's blue Mini parked in the driveway. Trust Ben to turn up unannounced, no doubt blissfully ignorant of the drama he had caused. The relief swept over them – until they learned it had been driven back from the Punga Cove bach by a mate doing Ben a good turn. The boys there had assumed Ben had caught a boat home, and they thought they'd better get his car back to him.

The next morning, Saturday 3 January, John Smart and Keith Reid set out for Furneaux at about 5.30 a.m. Gerald Hope believed his time was best spent at home, manning the increasingly busy phones. Over the next few days he stuck to that task, increasingly worried and increasingly busy, mobilising a growing army of searchers. That first morning, John Smart and Keith Reid wanted to talk to the water taxi drivers and as many other people as they could who had been anchored at Furneaux for New Year. John had heard that one of the Naiad operators was living on a boat in the harbour. They found him, but he wasn't able to help; he had stopped working earlier that night. None of the other Naiad operators they located had any information either. They couldn't recall seeing Ben and Olivia. So John and his brother-in-law looked elsewhere, and talked to many of the staff and guests still at Furneaux and the camping ground. They heard a lot of stories about kids coming off boats at all hours and putting up tents, but none of the leads pointed to Ben and Olivia.

They then went over to Punga Cove and found a group of the boys who had been staying at the bach with Ben. They were sitting on the jetty, and they had a boat, so John suggested they divide up the shoreline and search it. Again the result was nothing. By the time John went back up to the bach in the afternoon, the boys had packed up their gear into a boat ready to return to Picton. John picked up Ben's gear: his blue backpack and guitar case. The bach was locked up. On the door was a sign telling Ben that people were looking for him.

By early afternoon, a contingent of boats had also arrived at Furneaux carrying the police and a group of volunteers who had come to help search. A young recruit constable took a statement from John there and then at Furneaux. John had little to say. He recounted Ben's departure for Punga Cove, his meeting with Rebecca at Furneaux on New Year's Eve, the clothing that Rebecca had last seen him in – a green shirt that she had given him for Christmas, a light grey speckled sweatshirt, jeans, a fawn baseball cap – and the results of his own inquiries around Furneaux that day. Looking over the statement, John had just one point to add: 'I would not be concerned if Ben had gone off by himself but I am concerned because this girl Olivia has gone missing with him as well. He is a responsible boy.'

Troubled, but still in two minds about the gravity of Ben's disappearance, John Smart was impressed with the police's readiness to throw resources at the investigation. 'They took it pretty seriously, looking at it as a missing persons right from the start. They were interviewing as many people as they could.'

Gerald Hope was, however, increasingly worried, and increasingly impatient. The searching was getting started, but not as thoroughly or as rapidly as he wanted. As a worried parent, he believed he was duty-bound to chivvy the police along as much as he could. And his organisation was certainly getting results. By early on the morning of Saturday 3 January he had a team of searchers, which included two friends, helping police on an initial search of the greater Endeavour Inlet area.

Back in Blenheim, Gerald Hope had experienced an edgy morning with the police. It was to set the tone for many of his dealings with the inquiry staff over coming months. Steve Caldwell had come into the Blenheim Police Station at about 10 a.m. on Saturday to be briefed on events, particularly Rob Radcliffe's inquiries at Furneaux. When he phoned Gerald Hope to come in for a meeting, Gerald turned up with a plan of attack. Caldwell had his own ideas. He wanted to harness all possible resources, but he also wanted to make sure the search was conducted properly.

'I advised him [Gerald] to go home and said we would run the inquiry. But he had a lot of his friends involved as well. They wanted to go out and search. I had a talk with Gerald, and told him basically what happens procedurally with a missing persons inquiry, what we were going to do.' He gathered that Gerald had started with his own inquiries, which had turned up a lot of rumours about what might have happened.

'I conveyed to Gerald that we were interested in facts and we would be making a very methodical investigation, and told him what the options were, where we should head from here. He was happy with that, and went home, and subsequently kept ringing up every short while, which I can understand, because he was very anxious as to what was going on.'

Caldwell, like most people on the investigation, told himself that, whether he was being helpful or not, Gerald was first and foremost a desperately worried parent: 'No one knows how they will handle grief until they hit it.' But Gerald Hope's eagerness to be involved in the investigation, and to make sure it covered all the bases he thought were important, quickly became a sore point with Caldwell. 'At one stage I had to ask him if he wanted to swap chairs with me: "That would be fine, you can do the inquiry and I'll go home." Honestly, if we listened to every suggestion, we'd still be here investigating.'

The tension between the police, who had procedures to follow, and Gerald, who had his own ideas about what needed to be done, was never entirely resolved. But Caldwell's priority that Saturday was to assemble the team who went to Furneaux to begin searches of the area, including nearby baches. One of the team was Detective Dick Rolton, who was to play a big part in the inquiry in coming weeks, managing the fast-growing file of witness statements and other reports, and acting as the key liaison man between the police and Ben and Olivia's families. As well, a Department of Conservation team was called in to do a motorbike search of the tracks around Furneaux. Notices about the missing pair were sent out for broadcast on marine radio frequencies, and a press release was prepared. The media might not be interested in a couple of kids who were a day or so late back from their New Year break, but any publicity, it was thought, might turn up some leads.

On this, the first proper day of the inquiry, Caldwell's concern was to put proper systems in place and to try to ensure that the many volunteers Gerald was drumming up were not going on wild goose chases or, worse, getting in the way of what might be vital evidence. 'There were a hell of a lot of people wanting to be helpful – friends of Gerald's wanting to go out and do the search. The question I asked was, Where are they going to search, and what are they looking for?' Caldwell wanted to be sure police were in control, using the civilian volunteers properly.

'So we had to taihoa them at Picton.'There had to be some co-ordination. They had to know if they found anything, what were they going to do with it. The majority of them stayed, as they were told, but I understand a few definitely didn't. They took off out into the Sounds, looking for what I don't know. So we had those types of problems. Someone had to take a hold of things by the collar and get some organisation, otherwise it just ends up being a shambles with the left hand not knowing what the right hand is doing.

'I was getting rung from Gerald every 10 or 15 minutes saying he had another theory of where they are – there is a ship down in Fiordland at the moment that fits the description, or whatever. I made up my mind I couldn't deal with him and deal with the inquiry at the same time.'

Gerald Hope believed he was only acting as any concerned parent would in such increasingly desperate circumstances – passing on to police all the information that was coming in to him. Who could tell how much of it might be vital? It was primarily to deal with this flow of information that Caldwell detailed Dick Rolton to look after communications with the families.

An early problem, and one that stayed for much of the inquiry, was how much information police could pass on to the families. Caldwell wanted to be as frank as he could, complying with the police's information disclosure guidelines that were part of its victim support system. He had talked to the families about their going public that first weekend in an effort to elicit as much information as possible. But the agreement was that police would handle the media after that. 'Gerald came back to me and said, "Thank you very much, Steve," for what we had done with the media. "It went very well, and now we don't want to have anything to do with the media." So I rang all the media up and said the families wanted their privacy respected. Then bugger me days if I don't turn on the radio the next day and hear Kim Hill saying she's talking to Gerald Hope in Blenheim.'

Commenting on this situation much later, Gerald Hope believed there was no point in addressing most of the specific points raised by police; he had heard the arguments many, many times. But he still believed that though he may have made a nuisance of himself, it was a case of having to – in order to make sure that both the police and the media would take notice of what was happening.

As he saw it, the media were not attracted to the story until a small paragraph appeared in the *Sunday Star Times* of 4 January which was followed up by Andi Brotherston who, for television viewers, broke the news on TV 3 that night.

'My concern was genuine and I realised that if they had been abducted, a word which I used on several occasions, then time was vital for us in tracking down a boat which would have been heading off-shore. Therefore to whip up the public's awareness of the possibility of abduction, it was vital for me to communicate openly and genuinely with the media as I did.' There was no time, he believed, for a slow, considered media strategy. He had to get the information out, so the right action could be taken as swiftly as possible.

'In hindsight, the platform that TV 3 provided set the tone and tempo of how the media throughout New Zealand began to track progress as the police swung into gear and our families' plight increased. Our concern was well captured by the media and they supported us in maintaining public awareness. We knew that many people would be on holiday, perhaps with no newspapers available and not choosing to listen to current news. From the early days we realised that we had to maintain the public's interest for up to three weeks so that the several hundred people who were at Furneaux could respond to the police or directly through the families with information that may relate to where Ben and Olivia were.'

Gerald Hope remains appreciative of the 'genuine support' given to the families by the media and he is sure that the information that the news stories generated certainly provided the police with a lot of useful information. 'I know as a fact that without that reach into the wider community the final accumulation of evidence would have been very difficult.' Any parent can surely understand his desperation for action. Even police who were sometimes exasperated knew that Gerald Hope and the other family members were acting as any parent would, worried beyond belief at what had happened to their child.

Caldwell was worried about what this meant for the inquiry. 'I guess when someone, a member of the families, seemed to be obsessed with speaking to the media, you have got to be a little bit careful with how much you tell them.'

There was also the delicate issue of preparing the families for any potentially embarrassing information that might come to light about Ben and Olivia.

'The Smarts said to me that they knew that nothing would come out that embarrasses them, but it would be pretty strange if things didn't come out about their son that they didn't know. He was a 21-year-old. They didn't know everything about what he did or what he was up to. They accepted that. I mean, a teenage boy or a teenage girl doesn't come home and debrief mum and dad on what they did. It is just part of bloody growing up, isn't it? There were things that I did that my folks probably didn't know. And we can't pick our victims. We can't pick who we deal with, or who the offenders are. We've just got to go with what we have got.'

Once they had spent some time at Furneaux, the police team made something of a breakthrough. They, like John Smart earlier in the day, had made no headway finding the water taxi driver who had ferried Ben and Olivia on their last known ride. None of the regular drivers recalled anything. But eventually a member of the Furneaux staff remembered that Guy Wallace, who had been working in the bar on New Year's Eve, had helped out after the regular drivers had finished work. Guy Wallace had left Furneaux by now – he had ended his job there the previous day – but Detective Constable Andy Saunders located him in Picton, and Wallace could certainly remember picking up a pair from the *Tamarack*.

'The two people I picked up off *Tamarack* asked this other guy if he had any room on his boat, and he said jokingly to the girl that she could come on board but she doesn't have to bring her mate with her. This was said as a joke and there was no animosity at all,' Guy Wallace told the detective. 'The girl looked about 20. She had blonde hair tied up at the back and she was wearing glasses. She had a black handbag with her. She was wearing a black tee-shirt with a dark-coloured V-neck sweatshirt over the top. The guy looked about the same age. He had short dark hair . . . The two of them seemed like real good friends. They had been drinking but they weren't overly intoxicated. Before I dropped them off on this other yacht, I asked both of them if they were okay with that because they didn't know the guy.'

He said it would have been about 5 a.m. or just after when he left them, and he remembered the yacht as a blue and white timber ketch with round portholes. 'The guy on the ketch would have been about 32, about 5'9" tall, wiry build. He was unshaven but he didn't have a moustache. He had short dark wavy hair, and he smelt like a bottle of bourbon.'

That short interview, with its ketch and unshaven stranger, was to shape the inquiry for weeks. And that evening Guy

Wallace had some more information. Police had obtained a video of the boats moored at Furneaux, and when Andy Saunders showed it to him, Wallace was pretty sure the boat at which he dropped off the pair was next to a yacht called the *Spirit of Marlborough*. He also remembered that the man was not the owner of the boat. 'I remember asking him and he said that he was just crewing.'

By the end of that day, when police finished work at 11.30 p.m., they at least had a picture of Ben's and Olivia's last moments with a known witness. And they had circulated 'Have You Seen?' notices around Blenheim pubs and backpacker lodges throughout the Sounds. But the case was still wide open. Ben's and Olivia's parents had been pretty certain the pair hadn't just done a runner, and Caldwell had a gut feeling that something was badly wrong, but he still couldn't rule out less sinister explanations.

'You have that sixth sense, and, yeah, day one I had some concerns. There were a number of scenarios that we were faced with: one is that they were being irresponsible, doing a 48-hour elope. Maybe they were just in a tent onshore. We knew Wallace had dropped them off on this yacht, this bloody ketch, but they could have got off and swum ashore, rode ashore, or got onto another yacht.

'There was another possibility that they had drowned going ashore. A yacht might have bloody knocked them over on the bottom of the harbour. Maybe they were lost in the bush — there are a lot of mine shafts and that type of thing over at Furneaux. Or maybe they had been abducted; they had got onto a yacht, and they had been taken off and they were on their way to Tonga.

'Or maybe they had been murdered. There were all these sorts of things that you are working through, but it was important that I kept an open mind.'

Wherever they were, they were not on the run spending money. Dick Rolton was checking their bank accounts on an hourly basis, but the query kept coming back blank. The last transaction was Ben's a minute into New Year's Day.

'That was our big hope, that they were being irresponsible. There was some rock concert or something in Havelock, so you had to wonder if they had gone around there. We were hoping to get something on the bank card saying Ben had been to the Havelock pub,' recalls Caldwell.

The media publicity, pub notices and marine radio broadcast were starting to set off a wave of possible sightings, second-hand stories, and recollections from people who had been at Furneaux and suddenly realised that incidents they had brushed over or discounted might be significant. By the end of Sunday 4 January the switchboard at the Blenheim Police Station was becoming inundated, and staff were finding it hard to track every call. They knew that until they had firm leads, just about everything would have to be followed up.

The main thing police were trying to follow up that weekend was the boat Guy Wallace had described. Steve Caldwell remembers, 'I had him [Wallace] in here, to assess him, and he struck me as a genuine guy, nothing to hide. In fact I asked him, in case this was going to become an issue, to draw a ketch, because I actually don't know what a ketch is. I know what a sloop is, but I am not a boat person. "Right," he said, "I am not a very good artist, but I will draw it for you." And he drew a picture of the bloody ketch. And that was one of the ones that went out through the media.'

The police's revision of the two-masted ketch for a single-masted sloop was still in the future, but months later Caldwell was still cursing himself for putting out Wallace's description of the ketch. 'It slowed us down a lot,' he says. 'I know what a bloody ketch is now.' The issue of the ketch is clearly linked in Caldwell's mind with some public and media misgivings about how long it took for the inquiry to get started.

'In the old days, I am talking two years ago, they would let you get on and do your inquiry, and then if you got caned at the High Court or the Court of Appeal or by Detective Joe Karam or those other bloody wankers who get on the case, they would then have a go at the police. But now they virtually run a parallel investigation, and they say, Why are you doing this, why are you doing that? And because of the nature of a criminal inquiry, it has to be secretive. You don't bloody telegraph what you have got and what your tactics are. I think this is a watershed case, and I would just like to see someone get hold of it and say, Look, there is freedom of the media but there is freedom of bloody other people as well, including the police, to carry out their business.'

The weekend had proved one thing to Steve Caldwell: this was no ordinary missing persons inquiry, and it looked unlikely that the Blenheim police could handle it on their own. If he needed to call in heavy artillery, where would he turn? Until six months earlier, Marlborough had been part of the police's Region 4, which was based in Wellington. But the latest restructuring had assigned Marlborough to a new police district, Tasman, which took in the West Coast, Nelson and Marlborough, and had its headquarters in Nelson; and the head of serious crime for the Tasman district had recently been transferred to Hamilton. As a stop-gap measure for a couple of months, the district was being covered by a duty detective inspector in Christchurch. So Steve Caldwell's call went to Rob Pope, of the Christchurch CIB. His involvement was an accident of timing. A month or two either side of January and Rob Pope might not have become involved with a case that, he soon realised, would grow to become larger and more public than anything else in his career.

At the time, Rob Pope had other concerns. He was mowing his lawns in suburban Christchurch and looking forward to his forthcoming leave. He had booked a place for the family smack in the middle of it all – Waikawa Bay, the site of Picton's main marina and the base for many of the yachts that sail the Sounds. He listened to Steve Caldwell's concerns and agreed that the case didn't seem to stack up as a standard missing persons inquiry. He said he would have a talk to his own superiors on the Monday morning.

The pressure was building not merely for the Blenheim police. The Smart and Hope families, too, were receiving a lot of calls from people who thought they might have useful information. One of the calls that came that Sunday worried Mary Smart much more than the others. And it introduced to the Smarts a name they were going to hear a great deal more of. A friend of the family knew a boy who had been to Christ's College with Ben. The boy, Ed Sundstrum, had been at Furneaux for the New Year party with his girlfriend, Amanda Egden. They had gone home with stories about a 'revolting' guy who had been going on about sex and Prozac. He had given Amanda the creeps. The Smarts' friend said Amanda was going to call the police and make a statement, but it might be worthwhile for the Smarts themselves to pass on the information.

Ed and Amanda had sailed into Endeavour Inlet on the yacht *Frenzy* for the evening with a group of teenagers, mainly school friends from Christ's College, St Margaret's and Rangi Ruru. At about 3 a.m. they came across a guy called Scott, who was asking the girls to come out onto his yacht for sex and talking about Prozac tee-shirts.

'I didn't know what Prozac was at that stage,' Amanda recalled. 'I asked the guy if I could have a Prozac tee-shirt and he said, "Yeah, if you come on my yacht."' Later on he said he was planning to sail to Tonga, and Amanda joked that she could come along and help crew the yacht. 'What, no sexual favours?' he replied. When another girl asked him what his boat was called, his answer was, 'Whatever you want, sugar.' He boasted that his boat was the only double-masted ketch in the inlet.

The kids remembered the man as white, about 5'8" (170 cm), stocky, scruffy looking, slightly drunk and in need of a shave. Amanda remembered that he was wearing a blue denim shirt and jeans. He had tattoos on his left forearm, and some amateur tats on the back of his hand.

The next day Mary checked with the police. Dick Rolton told her Amanda had indeed called, and Mary asked if they had managed to find out who the guy was. 'Oh yeah,' Dick Rolton told her. 'That was old Scottie Watson. He's all right.'

In fact, Watson had already been identified on a list that eventually grew to 130. They were people who had a suspicious background, or who for any reason set off alarm bells, and who had been at Furneaux that night. Technically, they were all 'suspects', although there was no reason to put Watson near the top of the growing list. Talking to Watson at this stage was, as police say, strictly routine. As a boat-owner who had been at Furneaux that night, he would have been spoken to by police in any case. However, behind the scenes, some of the Picton staff who knew him were saying if there had been a problem at Furneaux, Scott Watson should be looked at very closely. Their early interviews had turned up stories of Watson making a nuisance of himself with women at Furneaux, so as well as his form, his behaviour on the night was beginning to mark him out.

On the day that Mary Smart asked Dick Rolton about the sex-and-Prozac guy, Rolton had already asked Constable Mike Lawson to visit Watson's home in Picton to get him to account for his movements over New Year. Scott Watson wasn't home, but the constable spoke to his father, and the next day Watson turned up at the station to answer the police's questions.

Mike Lawson put to him a standard suspects' questionnaire. Watson said he'd had a 'pretty heavy night' but the next morning he had woken up early and decided to sail out of the Inlet. Lawson found Watson's demeanour 'smarmy'.

'He had a confident appearance and it came across that he had nothing to hide. He gave answers to all questions on the questionnaire and never missed a beat. His reply to the question of leaving early in the morning was that it was quite normal and nothing to question.' Mike Lawson didn't notice whether Watson was carrying any scars or injuries that he might have picked up in a struggle.

While the decision was being made about whether outside reinforcements would be needed, the Blenheim team carried on with the inquiry, assisted by Nelson CIB staff sent over to help get it up to speed. It was still far from clear whether a crime had been committed, but on 4 January Steve Caldwell also put in place some victim support procedures which focused on trying to keep the families informed about what was happening. It was the first of what turned out to be daily conferences with the Hopes and Smarts. A yacht phase was also set up, to try to log all the boats that had been at Furneaux that night, with the aim of identifying and interviewing everybody who had been on board.

On Monday Rob Radcliffe and Andy Saunders were sent with a team to Furneaux again. They wanted to ask staff more questions and to inspect the Naiad. If they were really lucky, it might show up some fingerprints. But there had been far too much contamination in the days since New Year.

Steve Caldwell also called on the Wellington police superintendent, Gerry Cunneen, to ask for the police launch *Lady Elizabeth* to be sent across Cook Strait. If Ben and Olivia had fallen into the water, or been thrown, there was a chance they could still be down on the floor of the inlet, maybe snagged on an anchor or tangled in seaweed. Steve Caldwell wanted divers to do a preliminary search for them. The divers went down on Tuesday, but found nothing.

Meanwhile Interpol was told about the pair, and a Customs alert was put in place. The Air Force was asked to have its Orions keep a lookout for a ketch that might have sailed out of Endeavour Inlet on New Year's Day, headed in any one of a number of destinations. Tonga was the most popular of the early rumours, and Gerald Hope, at least, was keen that they try to follow that lead.

But most of all, the Blenheim team struggled to keep up with the media and public calls, and the deluge of videos and photos, many undeveloped, that began to flood into the station in response to a request that had been broadcast over TV1 and TV3.

'We didn't have a hell of a lot of staff,' Steve Caldwell said later, when the Blenheim station was returning to something like normal. 'We were just getting our systems sorted out, and when we went to the national media it just gripped the bloody public imagination overnight. We were getting inundated with phone calls – people had seen the ketch, it was sailing for Tonga, they had seen Ben and Olivia and they were in Hamilton. These things usually happen, but we were inundated, overwhelmed with public interest, which obviously translates into work for the police.'

One of the photographs that came in was a view of Endeavour Inlet taken by a woman at about 6 a.m. on New Year's Day. It showed many of the yachts moored at Furneaux; and a Picton shipbroker, who knew most of the local craft, was called in to make a start on identifying them. From Guy Wallace's statements, the police had a fair idea where the ketch would have been. It couldn't be found.

When he was first interviewed on Saturday 3 January, Guy Wallace had given Detective Constable Andy Saunders a succinct description of the man last seen with Ben and Olivia, and of his boat. The guy, he said, was about 32, about 5'9" tall, wiry and unshaved. 'He had short dark wavy hair and smelled like a bottle of bourbon.' The boat was a timber ketch – a two-masted boat – with round portholes. It was really old, blue and white, with a dark blue stripe along the side.

The same evening, Saunders talked to Wallace again and got a fuller description of the boat. Wallace said it was 38 to 40 feet (12–13 metres) long, with very thick railings along the side and a low cabin in the centre with a lot of ropes hanging around it; it was probably a ketch. But on what was to become a crucial point, Wallace was less than definitive: 'I'm pretty sure it had two masts.'

On Monday, Saunders was back at Furneaux talking to Wallace again. This time Wallace offered a much fuller description, and drew a sketch of the boat. He was in no doubt it was a ketch, describing it as an old design, probably dating from the 1960s, with about five to seven portholes with brass surrounds on each side. He described it as white with a dark blue stripe and a cream cabin. It had a bulbous transom at the stern, and a flexi side-rail with stanchions. Wallace added that he had been involved with boating for eight or nine years, including a lot of offshore racing and boat deliveries. 'I know different classes of boats pretty well,' he told Saunders. He also said the man had been wearing blue jeans and sandshoes, with a short-sleeved cotton Levi shirt, the colour somewhere between khaki and very pale green.

The next day Wallace was at the Blenheim Police Station, but he added little to his descriptions, except to say that the ketch had been rafted up in a group of about five boats. One of the other boats in the group was a Markline class, possibly called *Nugget*. He recalled that on the water taxi ride, when Ben had asked the guy if the Markline was his, he had said, 'No, it's tied up next to it but I don't own it. I only crew on it.' Wallace also remembered that the guy had been in the bar for much of the evening, drinking at Reg's Corner.

On that call to the station, Saunders and Mike Porter photographed Wallace's shirt because, except for having long sleeves, it was the same as the one he described the suspect wearing.

The last item on Steve Caldwell's de-brief notes for his part of the operation is for Tuesday 6 January: '1400 briefing, Rob Pope takes over.'

It was a briefing the families would always remember. 'I said to them,' Caldwell recalls, '"This is Detective Inspector Pope. As of today he is taking over the inquiry and it is now going to be run as a homicide inquiry." Now perhaps that was a little bit brutal because the shoulders dropped and everyone looked uncomfortable, but personally I believe sometimes you have got to be cruel to be kind. It's no use holding on to false hope when no hope exists. But it is very hard when you are a local police officer dealing with local people – sometimes you have to remove yourself from the emotion that goes on in the room. Your training kicks in, your experience kicks in, and you have got to be quite objective.'

Caldwell had known 'Popey' before the investigation, and professed relief at being able to hand the inquiry over to such a professional pair of hands. The investigation was growing virtually by the minute, and somebody had to take care of routine Blenheim business, after all. But the way the hand-over was pictured by some media rankled – and still does.

'Most of them arrived over here on the Monday, and they were quite bloody rabid. We got an editorial saying that police are sitting on their hands. Next minute it's the country yokels don't know what they are doing and the saviours from Christchurch are turning up. In small towns like Blenheim we have a very, very good relationship with the local media. It's built on trust. If you trust people, you sit down and talk with them; and the local media were in on the briefings and that type of thing right from day one. My view was that we were going to use them to get it out into the public arena as quickly as possible, so they had to be aware what was going on, both on the record and off the record.

'But then things changed when our friends from Wellington arrived. When you start putting people at arm's length, because there is no trust, what happened in very simple terms was the made-up stories. The media toddled off to Picton and made a nuisance of themselves up there interviewing witnesses, and when they couldn't do that they were interviewing themselves basically.'

Any police reporter would recognise Caldwell's point. Those doing the daily rounds soon get on a first-name basis with the police, who fill them in on all the background and supposition on the understanding that only 'on the record' material gets in the paper. The drill is often very blunt: off the record, this is what we reckon happened; on the record, this is what you can say, even if it's not much more than, 'Police are continuing their inquiries and are interested in talking to any members of the public who may have seen anything suspicious.' The system works for both parties. Police get the information they want into the public arena, and the reporters get something of a story on the understanding that, when the real break comes, they'll have it first. Experienced local reporters such as Tessa Nicholson, of the *Marlborough Express*, knew the routine well, and Steve Caldwell and his staff knew and trusted her enough to let her attend their own briefings, for background. But when a police story becomes a big story, and when a local story goes national, the unwritten rules don't work any more. Suddenly there are strangers from out of town, some of them quasi-celebrities, knocking on the police's door, and there's no way they are going to be given the inside running. Blenheim was about to be the unlikely centre of a media storm.

But now it was all somebody else's problem – Rob Pope's. For a start, Steve Caldwell continued to attend the daily briefings, but he soon slackened back to one or two a week and eventually not even that.

'I made a choice. Either you are in or out. You are part of the inquiry or you piss off. Life goes on, and I made up my mind; I made a conscious decision that, rightly or wrongly, I had to detach myself from the investigation and just let Rob get on with it.'

Pushed, Steve Caldwell will admit it was a wrench to let go of his biggest case, even if he was in charge of it only for four days.

'You know, Popey did an excellent job, but at the back of your mind it is quite hard . . . I left it in very capable hands. But it is difficult when you are running something. It is your patch, you've got a bit of ownership of it.'

Whatever else he did, Steve Caldwell left the inquiry one permanent legacy: its name. Early on, police realised they needed a name for an operation that might go on for weeks, maybe months. Steve Caldwell suggested Operation Tam. Staff said, 'What do you mean, Tam?' 'It's obvious,' Steve Caldwell replied: 'Tam, short for *Tamarack.*'

It was not, as cynics or reporters or clairvoyants suggested later, an acronym of 'Two Are Missing' or 'Two Are Murdered' or anything mysterious at all.

3

DIFFERENT PERSONS

WHO WERE BEN AND OLIVIA? The question was vital to the police, because it might help explain where they had gone, what had happened to them. But publicly Ben and Olivia became swamped by a media storm that transformed them into silent celebrities. They became different people, symbols who had to personify the innocence that was lost when evil intruded into the paradise of the Marlborough Sounds.

For months after the couple disappeared, a single photograph of Ben and Olivia became one of the most recognisable media images in the country. TV1 used it as the studio backdrop for its seemingly nightly *One Network News* reports on the case, and most media used the picture again and again in their coverage. In the photo, Ben is in sunglasses and a baseball cap worn back to front, gesturing towards the camera like he's having a joke with the photographer. Olivia, in a sleeveless summer dress, is smiling at the camera, but her body language is more turned towards Ben as if she's rapt to be with the boy of her dreams. The picture neatly captures one of the themes that made the story so compelling: they were a beautiful young couple and they had been cruelly snuffed out. Two people who happened to get together on New Year's Eve became one; they became 'Ben and Olivia'. It was beside the point that they weren't really a couple at all.

John and Mary Smart now have a framed copy of the picture in their home, given to them after Ben and Olivia disappeared. When the photograph was taken – at the Marlborough wine and food festival – Ben and Olivia had only the most fleeting of friendships. The Smarts didn't even know who the girl was. Mary recalled later that Ben had a huge bunch of friends staying at home for the weekend of the festival, and they were having him on about a girl. 'He's with this girl,' they told John and Mary. 'She's really gorgeous but she's really young.' The Smarts didn't think to find out the girl's name.

They also remembered an occasion when their family had been having lunch at the Wairau River winery, and Olivia was their waitress. She seemed totally embarrassed to be serving them, especially Ben. When she brought his meal to the table she turned bright scarlet and, Mary remembered, practically threw the plate down in front of him 'like a frisbee'. After she had left, everyone fell about laughing, but Ben was left in the dark, saying, 'What's going on? Who was she?' He had no idea what the fuss was about.

'Apparently,' Mary said, 'she's always liked Ben. But he never talked about her. So when police asked about them, we said, No, no, they'd never had a relationship.'

As two reasonably well-off kids in a small town, Ben and Olivia inevitably moved in similar circles. But when their disappearance broke, neither set of parents had any reason to think their children had more than a casual friendship, if that.

Gerald Hope, for one, didn't know much about Ben. He thought he had met him once the previous January when he had come to a party the Hope girls threw in the family's paddock, on their 'lifestyle' block in Grovetown. He had seemed a nice guy who was good fun and liked his music, and Olivia was clearly interested in him. But Gerald didn't think they had had any contact since then. Jan thought Olivia had liked Ben a couple of years ago, and she had been to his 21st, but there was nothing more than that. She certainly didn't think Olivia had planned to meet up with Ben at Furneaux. They must have just run into each other there. Besides, lately Olivia had been more concerned about the break-up of her relationship with a local boy. She had been to see him in Christchurch and there had been some anguished phone calls after the relationship ended, but they had talked recently and decided they were happy to be just friends. Before that, Olivia had been out with another Blenheim boy, but that had ended when he went to school in Christchurch. Her parents discouraged her from getting too involved with any of her male friends, saying there was plenty of time. Ben Smart had never figured in that picture.

Ben's and Olivia's parents had been talking to the police since their children were first reported lost. But on Tuesday 6 January, as control of the inquiry was passing from Blenheim police to Rob Pope's team, it was time for each of them to come down to the Blenheim Police Station to give full statements, alone, telling the police what they knew of their children, any pointers that might help to locate them and, bluntly, any anatomical details that could help if it ever came to having to identify their children's bodies. When mishap hits a family, few secrets are out of bounds and police try to trawl in as much detail as possible, hoping that a few strands might eventually lead somewhere. And at this early stage, when all options from elopement to foolhardiness to foul play were being considered, police wanted everything on the table.

Gerald Hope, whose interview came first, was 47 years old, and he managed the Marlborough Research Centre. He and Jan had been married for 25 years, and had two daughters, Amelia aged 19 and Olivia, 17. Olivia had just finished in the seventh form at Marlborough Girls' College and had been doing holiday jobs at the Wairau River winery and at Deka. He told Dick Rolton that she was 5'7" tall – he knew that because they had it marked on the wall of their home.

Gerald and Jan did not want me to quote the comments they gave to police that day. They felt that many of the questions they were asked were painful or unnecessary. And the last thing they wanted to be doing was to be sitting in a police station answering what they saw as superfluous questions.

Most of what he and Jan covered in their interviews was repeated much later when they had to front up to a crowded courtroom to answer the same questions, this time for the sake of a jury.

Olivia had left for Furneaux in high spirits and, as Gerald recalled, she had been wearing a greenstone pendant, in the pattern of an uncurling frond. It had been a Christmas present from her parents. She had taken no cash with her, because there was nowhere to spend it.

As far as he knew, she had no health problems, although she had suffered from tonsillitis in the past and had medication for acne. To the police, and in court, Gerald described Olivia as a bright teenager – sensitive and self-conscious as well as being assertive and outspoken. While Gerald believed her to be more trusting than might be wise – a trait the Smarts also identified in their son – he believed that if she was in trouble she would readily try to talk her way out of it. She was likely to try to get the last word in, or to walk away from an argument if she felt she wasn't getting the upper hand.

He could have been describing virtually any bright, strong-minded teenager.

In another room at the station, Jan Hope was talking to Raquel Hibbs, of the Nelson CIB. Jan was 46, born in England and now working as manager at the Wairau River winery.

As a mother, she could offer a fuller picture of Olivia's physical appearance and clothing. She described Olivia as about eight and a half stone, with shoulder-length blonde hair that she streaked with different shades of blonde. She was a size 10, and her shoe size was seven or seven and a half. She wore glasses for short-sightedness, and also had contact lenses which she had taken to Furneaux. She wore a brown Swatch watch with gold numerals and sometimes also wore silver bracelets, but Jan wasn't sure if she had these at Furneaux.

Olivia had started school at Tuamarina School and moved to Rapaura School before going to Marlborough Girls' College. Throughout her schooling she had lived at home, but she was moving to Dunedin in 1998 to enrol at Otago University. She was planning to study law, music composition, New Zealand literature, political studies and maybe a geography paper. She would live in a hall of residence, and although her sister Amelia was at Otago, and many of her friends were also going there, Olivia thought she would be homesick.

She had had a hernia operation when she was very young and suffered from glandular fever when she was in the sixth form. Just before Christmas she had complained of being tired, and her parents had wondered if the glandular fever was returning, but it had never been checked out.

As they later repeated in court, both parents prided themselves on close relationships with Olivia. She confided in them, even if she was prone to spar a little with them. Neither of them regarded Olivia as particularly fit or outdoorsy. She hated camping and liked the creature comforts of home – although, like many teenagers, she sometimes exasperated her parents with her untidy bedroom.

Jan was later to describe Olivia in court as a particularly bubbly girl, even if she could sometimes get grumpy and argumentative. Olivia and Gerald were so close in nature that the occasional sparring matches were inevitable. Olivia was close to the family and would ring home if she was ever kept away for any reason. 'She always kept us in touch with what she was doing and would let us know if her plans altered.'

In court, Jan had one word to describe Olivia: 'loving. She was very loving'. She was the type of girl who would ring her mother every day at the winery, as soon as she got home from school, just to tell her what had happened that day.

As Jan told the court, it was completely out of character for Olivia to be away for long without any contact with her parents. She would surely have been concerned, if only because she would have known how worried her parents would have been.

Also, she didn't like small places. She definitely would not have liked being confined in a boat. Her parents remembered taking her to a cave once and she had not liked it at all. She had hated the closeness of it.

After lunch it was time for Ben's parents to give their statements, Mary Smart in one room at the police station with Raquel Hibbs, and John in another with Dick Rolton.

Mary said she was 51 years old, and 21-year-old Ben was her only son, a middle child between two daughters. She described Ben as about 5'9", medium build, with short dark hair which curls when it is longer, and light brown eyes.

'He does not have pierced ears. He has no tattoos, but he has a small scar on his left eye below his eyebrow. I don't think he has any moles that would stand out and he does not have a birthmark.' He kept his fingernails short for playing the guitar, and had calluses on his fingers. None of his teeth were capped, but he did have some fillings.

He never took off his watch, which was silver, chunky and expensive. He also wore a greenstone pendant – a circle with the leather thong looped through the hole and tied at the back of his neck. And he wore a ring on his right hand, silver, with maybe an engraved star. As for his wardrobe, Ben went for a casual, young look: jeans, and tee-shirts with either surf or wine labels, and nearly always a cap back to front. He had about 10 caps, and Mary thought he was probably wearing his mustard-coloured 'Rip Curl' one. For the rest, Mary couldn't be precise. Some of his clothes had been returned, along with his guitar, pack and sleeping bag, but Mary wasn't sure what clothes were missing. According to Rebecca, he had been wearing tan lace-up boots that night, but Mary didn't think they were his.

She said he smoked Benson & Hedges Mild. 'He doesn't smoke much more than about five smokes a day on a normal day, but when he is out and about in town he probably smokes more.'

So far Ben sounded like nearly any casual young 20-something, but his early background was more unusual. He had started school at Picton Borough School, but then the family moved to Saudi Arabia, where John Smart had an engineering contract, and Ben attended SAIS International School, in Jubail. Back in Marlborough, Ben then spent a year and a half at St Mary's School, Blenheim's Catholic school, before more engineering work took the family to the Maldive Islands in the Indian Ocean. This time Ben did correspondence schooling before returning to St Mary's for another two years. He started his secondary schooling at Marlborough Boys' College until John's work took him overseas again. This time, Ben was given the option of staying at boarding school in New Zealand, and he chose to go to Christ's College. After leaving, he studied engineering for a year at Canterbury University but didn't do well and transferred to Christchurch Polytechnic, where he had just finished a two-year civil engineering course.

'Ben was a bright student but he was lazy,' said Mary. 'He was a school prefect and a house prefect at boarding school. He didn't really enjoy the academic side of school but he loved the social side of things.' He was also very independent. Unusually for a 21-year-old in the 1990s, he had already been flatting for three years. In fact, he was still paying rent on his flat because he was tied into a 12-month lease. 'If for some reason he had taken off and was going somewhere,' Mary offered, 'I think he would go back to his flat in Christchurch . . . but he doesn't have a key.'

Health-wise, Ben was no fitness fanatic, but he was naturally fit, his mother said. 'He does not play any sports but has played water polo, social rugby and snow skiing. He is a strong swimmer and windsurfer. He is not scared of the water and would have no problems if he was in the water. He has had a bit of experience with boats, and last year he and some mates hired a boat and sailed that around. I think he probably quite likes camping.'

Asked to identify any problems the family had had with Ben, Mary had to think hard. 'There was only one time two or three years ago where we had to have a decent talk to him about not helping around the house. We sorted this out, though, and things got back to normal.' Mary was confident that Ben had no emotional problems. 'Ben is a very happy person. He is always described by people as very happy. I have never seen Ben down in the dumps. I am sure he has been at some stage but I have never noticed it. He probably just goes a little quieter than usual. Ben does not have a problem with his temper and is really placid.' Mary added that his young cousins, aged between nine and 18, 'adored' Ben, and so did all her friends.

Mary was sure he would never contemplate taking off without telling anyone. 'If he had a problem, he would sort it out head-on and not run away from it.' Even if he had done something wrong at Furneaux, it would be unlike Ben to take off. 'He got caught for drink-driving a few years ago and he rang and told his sister, so if he had done something that he didn't want us to know about he would have at least rung Rebecca. He tells Rebecca everything.' But neither did Mary expect him to tell the family his every movement. 'I never expect him to ring me all the time and let me know what he is doing. I consider him to be an adult.' That was the basis on which he had gone to Furneaux, saying only that he would be back in time for work at his father's firm on Monday 5 January. Not only was he enjoying the work, but he was planning to go overseas at some stage soon and was keen to save money.

One unusual aspect of Ben's disappearance, Mary said, was that he had left his guitar behind at the bach. 'He plays in a band and would not have left his guitar behind if he was leaving the area. He would also have wanted a change of clothes if he had been going somewhere.' Mary said Ben was a very organised person, who planned ahead. For instance, he would always pack containers of water in his car for the drive down to Christchurch, and he was good at paying off debts and making sure he had paid bills such as electricity and rent at the flat before spending the rest of his money on drink and smokes.

But Mary had one fear for her son: 'I don't know what has happened to them but I know that if he was dropped off in the middle of the Sounds he would not know his way home, because he has a terrible sense of direction.'

Mary had struggled to keep her interview matter-of-fact. It was not a case of refusing to let her guard down, but of refusing to panic, even in the face of increasingly grim odds. John Smart, in his taciturn way, betrayed more of their pride in a loved son.

After giving Dick Rolton his own age – 58 – John covered much of the same ground Mary did, albeit in a father's more distant way. 'Sometimes he wears a cord with something on it around his neck. He does not wear rings, and nor does he have any studs etc. As far as I know he has no tattoos, certainly no birthmarks, no scars that I know of, no operations or things like that which would leave scars. I don't know of him having broken bones, and don't know or can't remember him having been x-rayed.'

John believed his son was reasonably fit. Although he wasn't playing any sports, he occasionally went for a jog with friends, and he was planning to play touch rugby and tennis this year. During the family's first stint in the Maldives Ben had persevered for months and become a skilled windsurfer. Second time there, he had done a scuba-diving course.

'Living on the Maldives he gained experience travelling on small boats, mostly launches. He has had limited experience on yachts locally . . . and his geographic knowledge of the Marlborough Sounds on water would be very limited. He would have no knowledge of the Pelorus. I think he knows how to steer a boat, but he has not had any experience with outboards.' John echoed Mary's assessment of Ben's poor sense of direction: 'I have no idea of his bush sense but he has no tramping or hunting experience.'

He described his son as gregarious. 'He has many friends, he relates very well to people of all ages and backgrounds. He makes conversation very easily, and he's not moody or short-tempered. He's a very laid-back, relaxed sort of person.'

John thought his son's big interests were pop music and guitar playing. 'He is a good guitarist and singer.' Ben was making reasonably good money from his band, Exit, which had played at pubs like Paddy Barry's in Blenheim and the Carlton in Christchurch, and at school functions including the Christ's College ball, the St Margaret's ball and Cashmere High's dance. The band was booked to play a 21st in January.

John said the family had sometimes worried about Ben's drinking since he left school. 'He doesn't drink during the week but often drinks far too much socially. We have spoken to him about our concern, but he just brushed it off as though we didn't know what we were talking about. When he is drinking his nature doesn't change. He doesn't get aggressive, he just gets this silly grin on his face.

'I don't know about cannabis; I have never seen any signs of it. But Mary seems to worry about that sometimes.'

John said he and Mary had earlier been worried about Ben's lack of application to his university studies. But they had been pleased with how he had responded to his failure at university. He had decided to make his own way through polytechnic, without financial support from his parents, and had really applied himself to his study. He was expecting his final results to arrive in mid-January.

'He has matured and seems to know what life is about. I believe I have a good relationship with Ben. He is happy to work with me and I am really pleased to have him with me.' They hadn't spent a lot of time talking. 'We probably don't get that much time together. When he is alone he is usually playing the guitar or composing songs. He has so many friends and is on the go all the time with music. He and Mary get on very well, apart from the odd problem with cleaning his room. We are very proud of him because he has a heart of gold. He's a well-rounded, good person, with a generous nature.'

John said Ben was reliable – he might stay away overnight sometimes when he was at home, but he would let the family know where he was, if not beforehand then certainly the next day.

'In this situation we are in, I am sure that if Ben had the ability to contact us he would. And given that he was last seen with Olivia as well, he would be doubly conscious of her parents' concern.'

Did those four interviews sum up two young lives? No parent can capture a couple of decades of their children's lives in an hour or two. Besides, they weren't trying to. They just wanted to give the police something to go on, to help them find Ben and Olivia and bring them home. They had described two healthy, well-adjusted young people who relished good company: at worst, Ben maybe liked a drink a little too much, and Olivia tended to be stubborn and self-centred at times. But if they were faults, they are traits that were shared by most kids their age. They didn't remotely begin to explain why or how they had suddenly disappeared.

Months later, long after they had told the police everything they could think of about Ben, John and Mary Smart were still coming to grips with the gap in their lives.

'When I think about him, and I'd never thought about this before, I don't think I've ever met such a happy person,' Mary said. 'He simply was never ever down; never ever moody or down.' That could sound like the sort of generous, selective memory we hold about loved ones who are gone, but to Mary it was a genuine, cool-headed assessment of her son. 'It's something that you don't ever think about when you live with someone like that. I think if you asked all of his friends, Ben would never have had a day when he was in a bad mood, would he, John? He was just very even or funny – always funny.'

She remembered a time they had returned home after Ben, at home alone, had thrown a party for his friends that left some damage around the house. They confronted him about the cigarette burns, the holes in the wall.

'He shrugs and says, "It wasn't me. What are you going to do about it?" Maybe it was infuriating at the time; looking back it was, well, Ben – easygoing and not one to bear a grudge or expect one to be borne against him. So you say, "You should take more responsibility for your friends." He shrugs and smiles. And that would be the end of it. Whereas girls slam doors and shout and scream at you.'

Mary was flicking through his CD collection as any parent might: 'Awful music – U2, Lenny Kravitz, Pearl Jam, Oasis, what was the one he was going to see in January, Radiohead?' But his parents saw that to Ben they had been more than a soundtrack to a crowded life, and instead a source of personal inspiration. He'd spent hours listening to them, and tried to take their lessons to his own band.

To John, Ben's big turnaround in the last couple of years had been in his attitude. Just as he'd tried to learn what he could from his music, he had also found a new seriousness in his study.

'That first year at university, when we were away overseas, I suppose you'd say he'd been living quite a carefree life. I don't really think he understood how hard you're supposed to work at university. But when we came back and he hadn't passed at Ilam, I said, "Look, what are you going to do now? Do you really want to be an engineer, or do you want to do something else?"' And Ben had surprised his parents. He said he did want to continue with engineering, and he wanted to do it under his own steam. 'He wanted to be independent financially, so he got a student loan and he went to polytechnic, and he did work well at polytech.'

John had been able to assess how much Ben had picked up at polytech since Ben began working with him in December. 'Other people had told us, but you never can be sure how hard they are working, so I sort of held back on congratulating him. But I did notice the work he was doing for me – I was very, very happy with the quality of it in an engineering sense. He was doing drafting, helping with survey work, structural calculations for retaining walls, steel or concrete beams, that kind of thing. His work proved to be very useful, a better standard than I expected. So his training had been very good.'

And Mary had discovered something else about her son. After he had gone missing, she and John went through his things, looking for clues that might point to where he could be. 'We got his songbook out and on the front of the songbook was written "Olivia" with a telephone number – weird, wasn't it?' Maybe Ben and Olivia were nearly a couple after all.

4

LAUNCHING TAM

WHEN HE WAS CALLED INTO the investigation, there was, according to Rob Pope, a 'rich hinterland of inquiry' to be worked over. What that meant was a huge canvas that was all but empty of real places to start from. 'From my experience,' Rob Pope observed as the inquiry was at last winding down, 'this is the least amount of evidence that's been presented to me in terms of where to start.

'If you look at a lot of the homicides we deal with – and we are talking homicide – often they leap up and hit you between the eyes. Others take some time to actually locate what's happened or where the offender is. Here, because of the massive amount of inquiry work needed, that process stretched out over months as opposed to days or weeks. There have been instances in the past where you've only got one starting point, but normally you've got supporting evidence that leads you more quickly to the old pot of gold.'

At the outset of Operation Tam there was no physical evidence, no crime scene, no weapon and, of course, no victims on hand. Instead, conspicuously, there was their absence. 'It was quite obvious that the one starting point was that the kids had gone to Furneaux for New Year's Eve and they were last seen boarding a boat in the early hours of the morning. And that was the sole starting point, really.'

When he got into work at the Christchurch Police Station on Monday 5 January, Rob Pope took his boss, Detective Superintendent Jim Millar, through the facts as Steve Caldwell had outlined them in his phone call. They agreed the case sounded worrying. They decided Pope should get up to Marlborough immediately to look at the file and decide whether police had a serious criminal investigation on their hands. Rob Pope joked that he wouldn't mind a couple of days sitting in the Blenheim sunshine, but sensed as he said it that the case wasn't quite going to pan out that way.

He was in Blenheim by the end of the day for a full briefing from Steve Caldwell. First off, he wanted to get an idea of just how serious – and how big – the case could become.

'Is it, first of all, a missing persons inquiry or is it a criminal investigation? Second, is it within the local policing resources to deal with it? Quite clearly, after the briefing, it wasn't.' A potentially vast investigation loomed. 'When I looked at it, we had a large number of boats and occupants that needed to be identified. We had a large number of "witnesses" at Furneaux Lodge on the evening, many of whom were known and most of whom weren't. They were a very itinerant population – they were there and then they were shot, gone back to points north and south.' And of course the police had to try to find Ben and Olivia.

Like the rest of the country watching the story unfold on the news, police still hoped they were alive. But if they weren't, Rob Pope decided on that Monday to launch a formal suspect phase to the inquiry. Without prejudging the situation, it was unlikely Ben and Olivia were just missing. Their disappearance leaned more towards criminal foul play, Pope believed. Conceivably, it was just a case of accidental mishap – but it was difficult to see how both Ben and Olivia could have disappeared accidentally. One person could fall overboard and drown, but could two?

'If there is criminal foul play involved, you've got to be in at the ground level,' says Rob Pope. 'Otherwise you lose a lot of valuable time and evidence, and the momentum of the case. It doesn't connote any sort of particular emphasis on an individual or groups of individuals. It's just that you will always get a large number of people who are nominated or come to our attention. We needed to begin working through these systematically.'

Within hours of arriving in Blenheim, it was clear to Pope that the case was going to require a large number of staff. He sent that message through to Jim Millar and to Dave Haslett, the detective inspector responsible for administration with the Christchurch CIB. Overnight, he tried to calculate exactly how many staff he would need, and how to bring some semblance of order to the flood of information that was beginning to flow in.

'You always get this havoc and mayhem in any inquiry in the initial stages, and the bigger the inquiry the more protracted the chaos is until things settle down. That's the biggest imperative in any large investigation – to get it under control as quickly as possible. Policemen are no different from any other individuals. If you know where you're going, it's much easier to get there.'

In the morning he called Christchurch and said he would need about 50 staff. Then he set about the difficult job of kicking off the inquiry on another policeman's patch, which meant contending with both the sheer logistics and local pride. 'You've got to be sensitive to that. Every policing district has its own pride in dealing with crime. But this was a distinctly different situation. It was quite obvious to anybody that it was well beyond the local resources. I think they were quite pleased to see us. When you have 14 staff working in a room probably three-quarters the size of this one in the Blenheim station, it was just chaos. They were doing their best, but they were just getting overloaded. There was so much information coming in, in the early stages, everyone wanting to help, and the systems were just not geared up to meet that incredible overload of information.

'Blenheim is a pretty sleepy sort of town in terms of major crime. They're not used to the systems that we operate on a regular basis in Christchurch. So that did create some initial difficulties in terms of trying to dampen down the chaos while at the same time maintaining at least the vestiges of an inquiry. You're trying to get the inquiry base up and running, get your staff in. Really it didn't kick in completely for about seven days.'

At the beginning Pope made two important decisions. He wanted a stand-alone inquiry, quite distinct from the local station's day-to-day operations. 'Crime doesn't stand still just because you've got a big inquiry on your hands. They needed to be able to get on with their work.' And he asked for John Rae as his second in command. Pope had worked with the detective senior sergeant on a number of cases, including Pope's biggest so far – the so-called 'poison professor' case, in which Christchurch scientist Vicky Calder was eventually acquitted on a charge of poisoning her former love, Professor David Lloyd. Pope and Rae had built up a strong working relationship.

'The most pivotal man in any inquiry this size is the 2IC, and John Rae is an absolutely superb bloke. He is the person who has to read every piece of paper, every little bit of information, and just keep the inquiries ticking over. Whereas I'm very much there as the co-ordinator and director and delegator, on a macro level, looking at the main issues and trying to keep the direction of the inquiry heading in the right way.'

To deal with the potential for bruised local egos – and to make the most of their local knowledge – Pope appointed a couple of Marlborough cops to key positions in the inquiry. Dick Rolton was put in charge of managing the file, keeping tabs on all the information flowing in and preparing it for the day, a long way off, when the prosecution would take a charge to court. And Mike Porter, the young Picton constable who had been on duty on New Year's Day, was made the analyst. It would be his job to sift through the information, looking at it from every possible angle for threads that might have gone unnoticed but which could conceivably be vital.

Early on, Pope and Rae faced a practical issue: where to base the inquiry. Normally, investigations are run as close as possible to the scene of the action. But Furneaux itself was out of the question. Accessible only by boat or walking track, it was too remote, and most of the New Year's players had moved away. Picton would have been suitable because many of the inquiries were centred there, but there was no appropriate building. That left Blenheim. If Operation Tam worked out of the station, it would need to take over an entire floor of the building, displacing normal operations. Preferring the separation, the team decided to set up headquarters in a disused community police station on the other side of the town centre. It had computer cabling already installed, but not much else. The Air Force and the Marlborough District Council supplied a truckload of furniture from the local Woodbourne Air Base and the council's supplies.

'The next three to five days most of the energy went into establishing the physical location, getting our rooms made up as best as possible, making the most of what was a far from ideal building. Just the sheer heat that was generated in there was awesome really. You had staff working very, very long hours in extremely hot conditions. It was very, very tiring,' Pope says. 'But you've got to cut the cloth according to the material you've got.

'There's other things, like people coming in to offer information, so we had to have a reception area. We had to have a secure area, where you can lock evidence and information away as best as possible. We had a bit of a rec room, which was very, very small, just where blokes can go and have a coffee. It was a far from an ideal base but it was adequate for our purposes.'

For getting around the Sounds, the operation worked out of the marina at Waikawa Bay, just up Queen Charlotte Sound from Picton, where Pope had been booked to come on holiday with his wife and children. They did join him there for a while, but it was hardly the break they had planned.

Although the disappearance of Ben and Olivia was still a mystery, John Rae quickly established the standard 'homicide pattern' for the investigation. 'It's something that's taught on the induction course, the detective course. When you have a major inquiry, the organisation for the investigation team is set up pretty well the same every time.' The investigation is divided into 'phases', each normally headed by a detective sergeant. But Operation Tam hardly fitted the normal homicide pattern because there were no bodies and, for the crucial early stages, no scene of the alleged crime. So the main early focus was on the search phase, the yacht phase, the witness phase and the suspects phase.

From the start it was clear to Pope and Rae that Operation Tam would have to be set up as an electronic file, with everything entered into computer files. So the Christchurch team brought in their serious crime system, which is usually set up on the third floor of the Christchurch station. It used the National Incidents and Crime Database (NICD) system, which police know as 'Nicked' from its acronym. Most of the Marlborough staff (who were used to the Plexis system in operation for the Wellington region) and many of the others brought in from other regions were not familiar with it and had to be brought up to speed. Rae, however, was most familiar with the NICD system, and had no doubts about importing it.

'All the information coming into the base – hand-written job sheets, hand-written statements, some typed statements on

Plexis, some typed statements on Word, depending on what particular police stations use – came to me. I read all the paperwork and gave it to the file manager to file. We only had 11 computers, which was a bit of a problem because we needed machines for the typist, the systems manager, the OC file, myself and obviously the staff. We did strike quite a few problems with making sure all the equipment was up to scratch, but they were all dealt with, so we had a system that was up and running and available.'

At the outset, the priority for the investigation was on two key phases – witnesses and boats. Detective Sergeant Dave Harvey was put in charge of the 20-odd staff whose job it would be to establish the names and addresses of the hundreds of people who had been at Furneaux that night, or who might have had contact with Ben and Olivia. The aim was to talk to every one of them. Wayne Stringer, from Nelson, was in charge of the boat phase which the Blenheim police had already launched. His aim was to identify and talk to the owners or occupiers of every boat in Endeavour Inlet that night.

At lunchtime on Wednesday 7 January, Rob Pope assembled the team for a briefing on what had been established in the week since Ben and Olivia had disappeared. Detective Sergeant Stringer outlined what appeared to be the facts. The couple, he said, had gone ashore at Furneaux Lodge on New Year's Eve and had a good time, before returning to Olivia's chartered yacht, the *Tamarack*, at about 3.30 a.m. There was the argument on board about the lack of berths and then the short ride on one of Furneaux's courtesy water taxis piloted by Guy Wallace.

'Olivia Hope asked him if he knew of any accommodation, and one of the passengers suggested they stay on his yacht. The couple have not been heard from or seen since,' Stringer told the briefing. 'We have yet to establish the yacht which is very unusual, and we have yet to establish the person who offered accommodation.' He described Ben as a good musician but 'apparently a hopeless case on the booze'. Olivia, he said, was 'emotionally up and down' and perhaps a bit spoilt. But they were both responsible kids who would be very unlikely to disappear for a day or two without calling mum and dad.

Pope told the briefing that until the previous day the case had been regarded as a missing persons inquiry, but now, he said, foul play couldn't be ruled out. 'It may be a natural disappearance, or accidental, but at this stage it is leading more towards suspicious circumstances.' He reiterated the gaping hole in the middle of the information that had been assembled – the lack of any information about the boat Ben and Olivia were last seen boarding. Wayne Stringer and his team were working through identifying the boats that had been at Furneaux on New Year's Eve. Many who had been there overnight had taken photos and videos, and with the help of a surveyor police were able to map the position of all the boats in the inlet, both on the evening of 31 December and early on New Year's Day. But none matched Wallace's description. There was one conceivable explanation: if the ketch had been there, it arrived late and left the inlet before dawn.

The unknown ketch was the best lead the police had to go on, and they released a 'suspect yacht profile' based on Wallace's description.

SUSPECT YACHT PROFILE

TYPE:	Ketch (double-masted yacht).
LENGTH:	38' to 40' (approximately 12 m).
CONSTRUCTION:	Traditional wooden ketch – 60's design.
FEATURES:	White hull, blue stripe along side below deckline, above waterline.
	5–7 portholes – brass surrounds – per side.
	Double-ender – canoe bow stern.

Bulbous transom (stern of vessel).
Flexi side-rail – stanchions running
alongside.
Blue gunwale belting strip along the length,
located above deckline.
Strip was chipped.

Pope, however, insisted in a press release that the ketch was not the only line of inquiry. It was just one aspect of it, and police were 'keeping an open mind as to Ben's and Olivia's whereabouts', he said.

'This is not a homicide inquiry but a major inquiry because foul play can't be discounted. It is now seven days since Ben Smart and Olivia Hope were last seen and we obviously have grave concerns for their safety.' He thanked the public for their response to police pleas for information – 'sightings' of the ketch and other findings such as a sleeping bag, a backpack and the smell of 'something dead' in a stream on the Queen Charlotte Walkway were flooding in – but he cautioned against any expectations of a rapid result.

'The enormity of the inquiry can be understood when it is realised that there were over 2000 people in the Furneaux Lodge area on New Year's Eve, and over 140 boats, all of which need to be located and identified to establish where people were and what happened.' He ended his statement with the recognition that 'this will probably be a long inquiry'.

It was already becoming a very broad inquiry. By Thursday 8 January, 60 of the boats that had been at Furneaux had been identified. Interpol and Customs offices throughout Australia and the Pacific Basin had been alerted. Amateur radio groups were asked to listen for any calls, and to alert their colleagues around the Pacific. And Pope had started what was to be a long communication with authorities around the world for satellite photos that might show the location of the mystery ketch in the

Sounds or, by now, more than a week's sailing time away. But the data from weather satellites was useless because the resolution was nowhere near good enough, and other sources reached a dead end.

The more mundane work of searching the beaches and walking tracks around Furneaux was also under way. That day they covered the shoreline from Punga Cove to Furneaux, but nothing relevant was found. The next day the searchers concentrated on the track from Punga through to Tawa Bay and back to Furneaux on a more intensive search. A team of about 70 people was assembled, including police, Search and Rescue volunteers from Marlborough and Nelson, and Air Force staff. As well as combing the shorelines and tracks, they set about trying to cover baches, mine shafts and any other places the couple could possibly have ventured or been taken to.

Detective Dick Rolton, who had been given the job of being the main point of contact with the families, was trying to keep them informed while also gathering more information from them for forensic and background purposes. Anything from exam papers which showed Ben's and Olivia's handwriting, to diaries that might indicate their plans for New Year and beyond, was potentially relevant. Ben's car was searched extensively, but it yielded no clues.

The massive media interest was generating a growing tide of information from people who thought they might have seen something. One of the most intriguing that week came from a local, Ted Walsh, who ran Picton Water Taxis and had been doing runs between Punga and Furneaux on New Year's Eve. On 2 January he was coming into Furneaux when he said he and his wife saw a boat that matched the ketch. On the back of the deck was a young blonde woman whom he later thought might have been Olivia Hope. She had the same stature and build. Walsh saw nothing untoward with the young woman's presence at the time, but he did wonder, 'What the hell's he doing out there in two and a half metre swells?' He and his wife each independently drew sketches of the ketch, which Walsh named as the *Astrix*. Police were definitely interested in talking to him further. But dozens of such 'leads' were pouring in, and most of them turned out to be dead ends.

In fact the investigation was making more progress than Pope or any of the team could have believed. Thursday 8 January was dominated by interviews with the two men on whom the case would hinge: Guy Wallace and Scott Watson. That day Pope, accompanied by Detective Sergeant Simon Moore, Detective Tom Fitzgerald and Detective Constable Annie McCornick, had arranged to take a boat trip up Queen Charlotte Sound to familiarise themselves with the area. On the way they called at the Bay of Many Coves to check out a sighting of a ketch. The caller had said he had seen one early that morning, heading for either Tory Channel or Picton. The police could find no sign of it. When they put out a call on the marine VHF radio for the boat, an unidentified male said it sounded as if they were describing the *Opposition*.

Out at Furneaux, police found Wallace in an agitated state; he was worried he was being lined up as the offender. Police assured him that at that stage it appeared his account was accurate and he wasn't being seen as a suspect. But Wallace complained that he and his family were being hounded by the media. Wallace was, in fact, becoming the case's first celebrity, and he was offering reporters increasingly detailed accounts of his boat ride with Ben and Olivia. He was told to leave media-handling to the police, and agreed that was the best course of action. There was just one reporter he was talking to, he said – the *Marlborough Express*'s Tessa Nicholson, whom he said he knew and trusted. The police told Wallace they would need him to come into Blenheim the next day to complete a compusketch of the mystery man, and that they wanted to interview him again because there appeared to be some confusion in his accounts, such as who had been on the Naiad with the mystery man on the first leg of the trip that later picked up Ben and Olivia.

Wallace said he was troubled by the fact that he couldn't remember the name of the ketch. He could almost see the name, he said, and it was an unusual one. If someone mentioned the name, it would come back to him. Moore asked if it was *Opposition*. Wallace rapidly replied that he knew the *Opposition* and had seen it in Ship Cove on New Year's Day. He had even rung police to report the sighting, he said, because it was somewhat similar to the ketch he had seen, and he wanted to clear up any confusion. While the ketch he had dropped the kids at had a wooden hull, the *Opposition*'s was steel, he said, and its blue band was wider.

In the growing confusion, two things were clear to police. Wallace was becoming increasingly, maybe infuriatingly, wedded to his description of the ketch he believed he had seen. And the details merely served to rule out any likely contenders. If the ketch ever existed, it seemed to have disappeared entirely from the Marlborough Sounds.

5

THE SUSPECT

AFTER THEIR INITIAL ENCOUNTER with Scott Watson, Picton police believed he was worth another talk. Watson had already been through the initial boat owners' interview with Mike Lawson on the Tuesday. But to Rob Pope at this stage, the interview was a pretty run-of-the-mill round-up of anyone who had been at Furneaux that night and who, because of their background, might warrant attention. Watson, at 26, had enough form to draw attention to himself, if not enough serious offending to point in the direction of the crime police were now considering a possibility.

When Detective Constable Taff Sanders met him at the Picton Police Station, Watson said he was on the dole and lived either at his parents' house in Picton, at his sister's along the street, or on his boat, a 26-foot (9-metre) steel yacht he called *Blade*. He told Sanders that he arrived at Furneaux at about lunchtime on New Year's Eve, alone on board the *Blade*. What followed sounded like a pretty ordinary good day out – pretty much like the time Ben and his mates were having at Punga, with a bit more drink and a somewhat anti-social edge. He said he rafted up the *Blade* next to a boat chartered by a bloke he knew and, after talking to him for a while, he spent most of the afternoon and early evening with a couple he knew from Picton and their two friends from Gisborne who were moored at Furneaux on their yacht. Between about 7 p.m. and 8 p.m. they took a Naiad water taxi to the Lodge, and Watson went back to his boat, drank some more rum and put on his shoes, and met up again with his mate Dave from the *Mina Cornelia.*

'I was pretty pissed by this stage. At some stage we got the water taxi to Furneaux. I can't even remember that. I think there might have been some pot. I can't really remember. I remember going into the bar and some guy tried to pick a fight with me. There was some punching and shoving and then some big guys came over and told him to piss off, and he did.' Watson said he remembered talking that night to Rick McLeod, the owner of Furneaux Lodge, but he didn't really recall talking properly to anyone else.

When he was shown the photos of Ben and Olivia, he said he didn't remember seeing them at all, but he did recall seeing the *Tamarack* during the afternoon and joking about all the pissed young people on board. When he read a description of the mystery man, Watson said he did not recall seeing anyone like that. He was also shown a depiction of the ketch, but said he couldn't recall seeing a boat like that at Furneaux. There was a ketch in the inlet that night, he thought, but it looked nothing like the description. 'I used to be a boat builder. I still sort of am. I take quite an interest in boats.'

He said that night he had been wearing blue jeans, black and white Bianchi shoes, a grey Ocean Spirit tee-shirt, and a grey jersey with two red stripes across the chest.

He said he caught a Naiad back to the *Blade* at about 2 a.m. 'It was driven by an old guy with a hat on. I was the only passenger. I remember he wouldn't let me on until he had parked the boat. He kept telling me to wait. I don't think I spoke with him.'

Watson said that once he was back on his boat, he jumped across to the *Mina Cornelia* to see if there was still any action going on. Everyone on board was asleep and the person he woke told him the party was over. So he went back to his boat, cooked up a feed of bacon and eggs, and went to sleep. He said he left the inlet at about 7 a.m. and sailed to Erie Bay to see a friend who was the caretaker there.

As the inquiry grew, about 130 people were at one time or another looked at in the potential suspect category. But something in that interview – Watson's manner, inconsistencies with other witnesses – began to spark higher interest among the police.

'At that point, don't ask me why,' Pope said later, Watson began to stand out. 'I still haven't quite worked it out, but it was quite apparent that Watson still had a few more questions to respond to. He was not identified by Wallace. All we had was that he had gone to Furneaux Lodge, and that previous comment by Picton police that he was worth looking at. He's the one who appeared to have the right sort of agenda and pedigree.'

To get the measure of that pedigree, Mike Porter, the Operation Tam analyst, began building up a suspect profile of Watson.

In any large inquiry, the analyst is pivotal, sorting all the information that comes in, but also sitting to one side of the investigation, testing any theories being developed and playing a sort of devil's advocate role in challenging the detectives' assumptions. Porter relished the role. It tested his policing skills, and allowed him to put his boating knowledge and love of the Sounds to good use.

'I was getting every bit of information that comes in, every bit of paperwork, every photo. I also did other things to assist the inquiry team. Where there is a hoard of information, I draw key factors out and present them to the inquiry team in the most usable way.'

With information coming in from a host of witnesses, it was Porter's job to match it all for inconsistencies, identifying who needed to be talked to again to build up a sequence and a timeframe of events. With hundreds of people who were at Furneaux being interviewed – many of them with a less than sharp recall of events that boozy night – his was going to be a difficult job. In the case of Scott Watson it was, first off, a case of putting together all the reliable information police could gather about both his behaviour that night and his background.

He had lived with his parents, Chris and Beverley, and his older brother and sister, Tom and Sandra, at Rolleston, near Christchurch, until he was about nine, when his parents built a yacht and with the family started to sail around the country. But when he hit his teens, he began a string of minor offending, and his parents kicked him off the yacht. He moved rapidly through boarding school, Social Welfare care and foster parents, until the fourth form at Ashburton College. That year was just about his only formal education. He hadn't regularly attended one school, and most of his learning had been in sporadic bouts of correspondence schooling. When he was expelled from Ashburton College, that was the end of his education.

From the age of 15, Watson was repeatedly charged with petty offences, generally related to theft or possession of cannabis. By January 1998 he had logged a total of 32 offences, including 11 related to cannabis, one for assault, and two for use of an offensive weapon. But he was hardly a sophisticated criminal. Most of his offences seemed to be unplanned, often while he was drunk or stoned, and he had put little effort into covering his tracks or avoiding the consequences. One arrest was for stealing $350 from his mother, an offence that she had reported to police. He had taken the money to buy drugs.

None of the rest of the family had any background of criminal offending. Of all the family, Watson was closest, by a long way, to his sister Sandra, whom he knew as Sandy. She was three years older than him, separated, and had children from her marriage. She spent a lot of time with Watson, and was extremely protective of him.

By the weekend Mike Porter had built up a one-page profile of Watson. He was 'a loner, described as having a chip on his shoulder, hates the world, surly, explosive temper, lacks social skills, drinker, smokes cannabis. Known to climb onto other boats at night, people on them or not.'

Some of the profile had come from Picton police, who had known Watson for a long time, Porter said. 'The Picton boys had previous knowledge of him of causing concerns – mainly threats to other people and that sort of thing. In fact some of the Picton staff said in the very early stages, even before anyone was being considered, that if something has happened out there, if we have a problem, you should be looking at this guy. He was the sort of person who would dominate weak characters. He wouldn't front up to big heavies around town, but he would put an image across of himself of fear and intimidation. People who create that sort of image are usually weaker sort of people. He had the characteristics we were interested in.'

Mike Porter soon realised his skills and resources were being stretched to the limit.

'Being an analyst in the rural area, you don't get usually into something as big as this. But speaking to colleagues in other areas, they said this was the biggest one police have ever had anyway. No one by themselves would have been experienced enough to handle all the information.' In other big cases, such as the *Rainbow Warrior* bombing, police assigned separate analysts to each phase of the inquiry. That would have been the ideal for Operation Tam. 'But because of staffing and resourcing, I was it, so I just had to hunker down and go for it. There is not much else you can do. Every single bit of paper came through me. I had support from Greg Sparrow, the analyst in Nelson, for a week, and right throughout the whole investigation I was able to call on the old brotherhood of analysts. You ring around and say, "Listen, I have got a problem with this; have any of you guys dealt with that before? Do you guys know another way of looking at what I'm seeing?"

'I had big problems with some of the computer software and hardware I had at the time. It was inadequate for the job – my computer was too slow. I contacted other people around the country and we got new hardware in.' Normally, police analysts use a purpose-made analysts' software platform based on the Link Notebook software. For any suspects such as Watson, it is designed to be able to throw up a graphic display of a person's movements and any associations with other people. But Porter found it wasn't coping, even with modifications. 'Normally you can just throw all the information in and it comes up with timings and schedules. But it was overloaded, it wasn't working on the systems I had.' So Porter started from scratch, compiling the information in Microsoft Word tables.

Porter's job had another unique obstacle. 'You didn't have the normal information that you would have after a homicide. You didn't have a scene, you didn't have witnesses, you didn't have any of that sort of stuff. Instead, you had all this quite incidental material – people who happened to have seen what was happening in the course of the evening, none of which is tied together. But you had to somehow tie it together.

'The best way was to try and be methodical, take your time, try to be analytical yourself. You sit down and look at the possibilities. I am the sort of person who likes to lay things out and look at them, and that is the way I did it, either on the computer, or talking to other people, sharing the information I had got, saying, "What do you think?" Because we are not meant to have all the answers; we are meant to question things, and put those questions out to the others.

'It was my job sometimes to stand up and say, "Hold on, what about this? Have you thought about this?" Probably the biggest thing was just reading everything and absorbing it, and putting it down onto tables and looking at it and re-looking at it. At one stage I had a timetable up that was about 60 feet long.

'Very early on, not knowing the two people we were dealing with, we were getting a lot of conflicting stories about their reliability and the way they would react. We had them going to Tonga; we had them camping in Pelorus; we had them in the bush somewhere. We had foul play; we had them heading off overseas, eloping and not wanting to be found. Out of all those, I had an open mind right at the start, and it wasn't until later on, once we had done a profile of both of them, and got more information in relation to the yachts and movements that night, that it was clear there was foul play involved.'

From the first week of the investigation, most of the alternative scenarios petered out, leaving Porter and the team looking at foul play, and looking at Scott Watson. The other suspects who were considered pretty quickly fell out of the picture because of their background, their alibis on the night or other factors.

'I think in total we had about 130 suspects thrown up at us. There were some that were well outside the loop but still had to be looked at. I looked at the type of people they were and whatnot. I focused tightly on a smaller group, and we probably had three or four in the early stages that were a bit stronger than others. Then, looking at each individual, one became more frequent, in our eyes, because of specific things he had done, and others became weaker.'

However, Watson was still far from being identified as the prime suspect. On the day of that first major interview with him, Monday 12 January, the Operation Tam team released two compusketches. One was based on Guy Wallace's description of the man he delivered to the ketch with Ben and Olivia. The second was based on accounts from bar staff and patrons at Furneaux, and showed a 'sleazy' man who had spent a good part of the evening in the bar and had made a nuisance of himself with some women. At the daily police briefing that evening Rob Pope reported that there were considerable similarities between the two pictured men, but that was as far as police could take it. 'Whether they are one and the same person we have yet to ascertain.'

In fact Watson was somewhat elusive to pin down as either mystery man. Pope reported to the briefing that Watson appeared to be a 'hassler' whom several witnesses had identified at the bar, but not the 'sleazo' in the compusketch. 'We can pretty much put him to one side at this stage without completely discounting him from any involvement,' Pope told the briefing. And while John Rae said that Watson was well known to Picton police as 'a stalker and a knife man', Simon Moore reported that Wallace did not recognise Watson and was adamant that his yacht was not the boat he had dropped the couple off at. He had seen photos of Watson's *Blade*, and said it was nothing like the ketch he had seen. He had mentioned *Maenz* as a possible name of the ketch, but he wasn't sure.

Guy Wallace offered the only hope of definitively proving that Watson was the mystery man he had carried on his water taxi, with Ben and Olivia, to the mystery boat. But he was turning out to be a difficult witness. He gave a long statement to Detective Tom Fitzgerald on the same day, but although he added a few more pieces to the jigsaw of events on New Year's Eve at Furneaux, it was hard to say how much he advanced the inquiry. The former barman described himself as unemployed now, his New Year job at the Lodge having ended. He said that since his previous statement he had remembered more details about the evening.

For a start he recalled the lone male he had earlier described seeing in the bar. He had been drinking by himself most of the night. 'I remember thinking to myself that he must have been bored just standing there,' Wallace said. 'He did speak to the odd person but not for any length of time. He was drinking bourbon. I served him on a number of occasions. He wasn't drinking heavily but more steadily. He appeared to be a fisherman or a tradesman by the way he dressed and his manner. When he paid for his drink he would just pull a fistful of money out of his jeans pocket. The money was just screwed up in a bundle. I remember that because it really pisses you off when you're working behind the bar and people just put screwed-up notes on the bar.'

Wallace then recounted the water taxi ride during which he dropped off a couple at the *Tamarack*, where Ben and Olivia got on board his Naiad, joining a man and another couple who had been on board for the whole trip and were to be dropped off last of all at Solitude Jetty. Most of the details were the same as he had earlier told police, except that this time he said that when Olivia got on she stumbled and fell, landing between Ben and Wallace himself. When she stood up and went to sit by Ben, the unknown man patted the pontoon beside him and said, 'No, come and sit here,' raising his eyebrows to Wallace, man to man, about the pretty girl on board.

Then followed the conversation about Ben and Olivia's lack of a bed and the stranger's offer of a berth on his boat. This time Wallace remembered the name as the *Maenz* or something similar. The stranger said the name two or three times, and Wallace remembered thinking, 'I don't want to know the name, I want directions.' This time Wallace didn't recall the stranger's comment to Ben that he didn't own the boat but was just crewing on it. Instead, he remembered the man saying he crewed on a fishing boat. Wallace said that when eventually they pulled up alongside the man's ketch, he thought what a nice, well-kept old boat it was. 'The ketch did not smell of fish at all. It was very tidy. The ropes at the back made me believe it was used for fishing. I have seen ropes like that before on other fishing boats. We had one very similar at Ohope Beach where I grew up. They use the ropes for tying marker buoys to long lines.'

Wallace thought there might have been a dinghy at the back of the ketch. This would explain why he let the three off at the port side of the ketch, rather than the stern where he normally would. 'Once they were on the ketch I said, "Are you guys all right with this?" I just had a feeling it wasn't right. They were both facing me and said, "Yes." I backed away from the ketch, went to the bow and carried on to Solitude Jetty to drop off the other young female and male on the boat. I didn't see whether Ben and Olivia went into the cabin or not. That was the last I saw of them.'

Wallace then recounted his next rides, ferrying people out to their boats. His last trip was to a fishing boat. After he had dropped the fishermen off, at about 5 a.m., he noticed that the ketch was still in the inlet. 'There was no life on it, no lights on or anyone on deck.'

That evening Tom Fitzgerald reported to the daily briefing that Wallace was making his own inquiries with Furneaux staff and others to try to pin down timings and other factors. Wallace believed the original timings he had given police were about an hour out, and he was now trying to sort them out. He was presumably trying to be helpful, but police hackles are always raised by a witness who tries to gather evidence rather than merely give it.

Detective Constable Sanders reported on his interview with Watson. He said he was making more inquiries with Sandy Watson, but she was unable to help much. She hadn't been at Furneaux on the night and did not think her brother was involved.

The rest of the briefing reflected the routine into which Operation Tam was settling a week after Ben and Olivia had been reported missing.

The ground search had focused on Endeavour Inlet that day. Progress was very slow and nothing of value as evidence had been found. The smell of something dead in a stream appeared to be nothing. A sleeping bag cover had been handed in to the inquiry, and would be shown to the families the next day. There were reports of an unknown, very drunk young blonde woman at Furneaux on the night but it was proving hard to identify her – there were no bookings for the tent that security guards had taken her to – and there was certainly nothing to suggest she was Olivia. In fact, Ben's father, John, appeared to have heard the same stories of a drunk blonde, and had talked to her on his first visit to Furneaux to rule out these descriptions as Olivia.

Wayne Stringer reported that 75 of the 82 boats seen in photos and videos had now been identified. He was most interested in a boat called something like *Mea New Zealand*, he said. 'This looks like our vessel. It was described by the water taxi people as being in about the same position as Wallace describes, so it all seems to tie in.' Stringer told the briefing his team was alerting Maritime Safety, Customs and Interpol about the boat to try to pin it down.

Simon Moore reported another suspect on the basis of information from Whangarei police. The man was facing several arrest warrants and had been involved in rip-offs in Ashburton and Wanganui in 1997. His name had come forward because he was missing and he seemed to have a habit of targeting overseas tourists, particularly women.

Dick Rolton had picked up some exhibits from Ben Smart's house and was planning to take a full statement from Ben's sister Rebecca.

There were still no sightings nor any information about what might have happened to Ben and Olivia after they boarded the boat.

Over the next few days, 15 more staff would be joining the inquiry, drawn from all over the South Island. They would take numbers to 44, and make Tam the biggest investigation in the

South Island for years. Satellite inquiry groups had also been set up in Christchurch, Dunedin, Wellington and Auckland to handle local interviews and inquiries. The investigation was settling in for a long haul.

.

6

SEARCHING

FATHER BARRY SCANNELL, OF St Mary's Catholic Church in Blenheim, spent his New Year at a cottage owned by his order, the Marists, in Ruakaka Bay, a couple of bays south of Endeavour Inlet along Queen Charlotte Sound. It was only when he returned to Blenheim on 4 January that he learned that one of the children of a parishioner had gone missing from a bay just across the water from his holiday cottage. Mary Smart attended St Mary's, and Scannell knew Ben and the rest of the family reasonably well.

'It was becoming obvious that something was really wrong here,' Scannell recalls. 'People were wanting to do something, because it was obvious that these kids hadn't come home, and it was most unlikely that they had just gone off, as I think may have been the initial thinking of the police even.'

Out of the desire to rally around the families came the idea of a church service. 'There was a real enthusiasm for doing something, but no one knew quite what to do. People felt helpless – these two kids had disappeared, and every day that went on the worse it looked. So we started to plan a little service and it became the first concrete expression of what a lot of people were feeling. It ritualised what was happening – people were able to do something. I mean, some people were obviously able to go out and take a boat and search, and there were people who were able to take food around for the Smarts and the Hopes. But many people couldn't really do much more. And because it gripped the whole community, this was the first practical thing that many people could do.'

The prayer service 'for the safe return of Olivia Hope and Ben Smart' on the evening of Friday 9 January brought nationwide attention to the small church of St Mary's, and touched many in the Marlborough community far beyond the Catholic parish. Many of those present had already put in days and days of searching the coastlines and waterways of the Marlborough Sounds, but the prayer service was concerned with another sort of searching – to find some meaning behind the apparently meaningless disappearance of Ben and Olivia. At best, that might provide clues to their return. At the least, the prayers might lead to some sort of acceptance of their disappearance.

The service did not begin well, however. The church was packed, and Scannell knew the numbers far exceeded the fire safety regulations. Even before the evening got under way, there was a real test for the rules. 'Two of the older guys in the parish were lighting some incense in the sacristy, and they set the fire alarms off. I was waiting, just about ready to start the liturgy. We were just about to have the opening hymn and the bloody fire alarm goes off. I couldn't work out what was happening. I really thought someone was sabotaging us. I finally worked out that they had set the detector off, but by then the fire brigade had arrived and they wanted the place cleared. But somebody told them, "Look, you can't clear this bloody place. There is a service just about to start." The fire brigade wasn't very happy with that, but anyway, we got going.'

The parish music group sang some songs; the chairman of the parish council offered some words; family and friends of Ben and Olivia led some prayers; and John Rae spoke on behalf of the police. He talked about how most of the Operation Tam members were parents themselves, so their hearts went out to the parents of Ben and Olivia. But few of the words spoken probably went as directly to the heart of the matter as the ancient Bible readings chosen by Father Barry Scannell. The first reading he chose was the Genesis story of Noah's ark lost at sea in the great flood, and the raven he sent out repeatedly to find signs of land. Then Noah sent a dove, which also returned fruitlessly. Seven days later he sent the dove again, and it returned in the evening, holding a freshly plucked olive leaf in its beak. Ceaseless searching can sometimes yield results. Scannell drew the parallel with those out looking for Ben and Olivia. 'And they will continue to do that until something is found,' he told the congregation.

His Gospel reading was Luke's story of Jesus and Mary losing their boy, Jesus, during their return from Jerusalem after the Feast of the Passover. For a day the parents assumed the boy was in the throng of pilgrims making their way home. But when it became apparent he was not in the group, the parents returned to Jerusalem and found their son still at the temple, talking to the elders. When they encountered him, Joseph and Mary were astonished. But Mary was also annoyed at the worry he had put his parents through. 'Son, why have you treated us like this?' she demanded. 'Your father and I have been anxiously searching for you.'

'Why were you searching for me?' Jesus asked. 'Didn't you know I had to be in my father's house?' But the worried parents didn't understand what he was talking about. 'Then,' Luke continues, 'he went down to Jerusalem with them and was obedient to them. But his mother treasured all these things in her heart.'

Scannell saw in the Gospel story a hint that Ben's and Olivia's parents might never fully understand what had happened. Life, Scannell said, was full of mystery and ambiguity: 'So many things are left unanswered. So much is mysterious. We have to pray for grace to live with the questions at this moment. We don't have a hotline, an 0800 to God, to provide the instant answers. The hard work needs to be done; the hard graft of the police and others who are placing their resources into locating Ben and Olivia. We must be patient. We must refrain from speculation and rumour. We must wait, and tonight, I am sure, is a reminder to each of us that we are not alone in our anxiety and in our desire to locate a son, a daughter, a friend.'

During the prayers and the songs, with everyone around her crying, Mary Smart felt numb. But it was, she said, 'a really powerful night. I actually felt it was. I actually felt that the power of everybody's love and concern was really strong. I felt uplifted by it.

'It was just prayers. Ben and Olivia's friends got up and talked about them – about half a dozen friends each. On the altar they had Ben's guitar and clothes, and Olivia's clothes. And they just prayed for their safe return, and their friends said what they wanted to say about them.'

John Smart, not a Catholic like his wife, wasn't at the prayer service. It was not that he didn't want to be. At one stage during those first weeks John had even half-joked to the priest that if he could bring Ben back he would become a Catholic.

Instead, John was out on a search of an altogether different spiritual nature. He was out over the Sounds with his daughter Rebecca and Gerald Hope in a helicopter, following a tip-off from one of the hundreds of psychics and clairvoyants who were flooding the families and the police with 'information'. John, Rebecca and Gerald had planned to be back in time for the church service, but the chopper had been delayed by high winds. The psychic had said she had never been to the Sounds, but she had described a bay in the outer Sounds with mussel rafts and a cross on a hill. Up on the hill, she said, there was a hut which had a view of the bay and the mussel rafts.

'Really,' John said, 'her description was quite amazing and we were able to pinpoint most of the features she described. But of course it led to nothing. That was just typical. But we did take these things quite seriously.'

Neither John and Mary Smart nor Gerald and Jan Hope were even remotely believers in the spiritual powers that some who approached them claimed to have, but they were desperate. They felt compelled to follow up any leads. They may have seemed weird and unbelievable, but what if there was something to them? One of these strangers might really know something.

'I defy anybody, no matter how scathing they can be about psychics, not to wonder if just possibly they might have had something,' Mary Smart says. 'I defy anybody in the same situation not to cling on to any little ray of hope. But you do. We knew that people were probably laughing at us. We were desperate people. We were desperate.

'They tell you silly things – like they got on one of these big boats with one of the crew. There were stories that guys had snuck them on board boats in the middle of the night and the captain took off in the morning and he's so annoyed. They would describe the boat, down to the last detail, and tell you where it had headed. Others told us they were definitely on land, and they would pinpoint the location.

'I said to the police right at the beginning, "Do you believe in psychics?" They said, "If we followed every psychic, we'd never ever finish an inquiry. We have to start in the middle and work out. That's the only way we know how to do it – eliminate every possibility along the way." But we felt we couldn't ignore them.

Looking back on it later, Mary Smart knew it was irrational to be following up all the psychics' leads, but she was stricken with grief and it was impossible to sort the sensible from the absurd. Maybe one of the leads would, somehow, prove to be genuine.

'Mostly they can't give locations. Some of them gave descriptions that would fit every bay in the Sounds. And they would just about all say they had never been to the Sounds. But some were very precise. I mean an elderly lady rang John from Wellington and said, "Look, I'm from Australia, I'm staying here with my two daughters. I had a dream last night and I woke up this morning and looked at a map of the Sounds and saw a bright ring in the Sounds around Dieffenbach Point. I have to tell you," she said. "I couldn't live the rest of my life if I hadn't told you." And of course, you take notice of dear old ladies who ring.'

'If they said they saw a bay with a light, for instance, you'd get out a map and look for all the bays with navigation lights,' John says. 'So we'd go around every navigation light, and look round all the beaches. There was another bay in Tory Channel where one person was very sure we'd find something. One came over from Wellington and went to a bay in Tory Channel and said, "In this bay, here." She could feel it. So we went and had some divers come in. We did a thorough search of that bay with the divers. But there was nothing.'

'How they had the confidence to go into this ludicrous detail and believe it and expect you to believe it, I don't know,' Mary says. 'But we did. They all do it in good faith, that's the thing. You actually can't turn around and say, "Look, just piss off." They do it in good faith. They're slightly different from me and you. But they do believe that what they're telling you is going to help you.'

'They honestly believe what they're telling you,' John says. 'I guess we held out a glimmer of hope for quite a few months.'

'Yeah, we did,' says Mary. 'We did. There was always that element of hope that perhaps they had got on a boat and gone to South America. It kept us going. A few psychics said that's what's happened. I don't think we ever believed it, did we, John?'

'Oh, I don't know. We had different stories that they had gone to Australia, India, South America, Tonga – all these different places. One was quite sure they had gone to Auckland and we'd hear from them by the fifth of April.'

Father Barry Scannell, too, was being besieged with people who claimed to have clues that could find Ben and Olivia.

'I had asked if anyone had any information that they couldn't tell the police, to let me know. I said to them, "The first thing you should do is give it to the police, but if you feel that you can't, then I would be happy to receive it and pass it on." There were lots of responses to me from people who were psychics, or who just had their own theories. They would write and draw little maps, or ring up and say they had woken up in the middle of the night with a strong feeling that the boat is here.

'I don't know whether all this was particularly helpful to the families, but the one thing I do know was that the Smarts were so generous in listening to these people, because they were really holding on – especially John – holding on to every bit of information. I remember one psychic guy from Nelson or Takaka or somewhere. He was there for two or three hours. John just sat patiently with him and listened. I think John had a lot more tolerance than Mary for that sort of thing.'

Scannell knew that, as a priest, he was on tricky ground calling for people to come forward to him with information. 'If someone had come up and said, "Well, yeah, I did it," that would have been a real dilemma. If someone had come to me with something in a confessional-type situation, certainly I wouldn't have been able to use it. But I certainly made it clear that I would only be passing information on with their permission. But nothing of any substance came to me. There was plenty of information, but it was just basically from people who were well intentioned but who were just going on their own psychic energy.'

At Operation Tam, the police took a pragmatic view of the clairvoyants.

'We had over 200 psychics come forward with information,' says John Rae. 'Some of it was so broad it could never be checked. Where they had a vision of two bodies being buried in sand by two trees in a bay in the Sounds, it's totally impossible to check. But if somebody drew a map and put X on it, we'd go and check it. They had different grades in terms of reliability, and that determined the priority we gave them.'

In the early days of the search, both the Hope and Smart families also hoped that more orthodox avenues would lead to valuable information. So although they were to varying degrees uneasy about it, they went to the media, talking to television, radio, magazines and newspapers in the hope that they might spark someone's memory or conscience.

'We're not media people,' Mary Smart says, 'but we did that initially because if, in fact, Ben and Olivia had been abducted – and we never thought for one minute that they'd eloped – we wanted them to hear us. It was to our benefit that it was made very public.'

That avenue, too, turned up nothing, but John and Mary, almost alone in the case, did not come away disenchanted with the media. 'We have no complaints at all. They were very kind to us.'

Throughout early and mid-January, the main aspect of Operation Tam that featured on the news and in the headlines every day was the searching – both the efforts organised by the families and the police's official searches. For Rob Pope, the search phase of the inquiry was 'extremely intensive and very resource-hungry. But it needed to be done. It needed to be done on two grounds: one, to exclude the possibility that Ben and Olivia had met some accidental mishap and to corroborate criminal foul play. And, importantly from the families' and our point of view, to actually locate the kids. Backing it up, you had the private searches which Gerald Hope was organising. So you had the Spanish Armada sometimes out there. It was quite enlightening.

'All the baches were searched. All the mine shafts were searched; all of the walking tracks, 10 metres each side right through the Queen Charlotte Walkway. We did constant aerial searches of all the coastlines and about 80 specific spot searches, as well as an armada of private searching. In addition, there was the naval searching later, with the deep-sea sonar. We covered virtually 2 square kilometres of the Endeavour Inlet. All of which has gone to prove that we've expended an inordinate amount of time and located absolutely nothing of significance.'

John Smart and Gerald Hope, with help mainly from a couple of Gerald's friends, were meanwhile following their own leads.

'We had 30-odd small boats and each day we gave them an area. We pretty much covered the whole Sounds like that,' John Smart says. 'And we did it several times. Quite often we had large turnouts; sometimes we just went in smaller parties. We looked at pretty well every bach in the Sounds. For those first few weeks we were talking to people about where the hell this ketch had gone. We were talking to everyone about ketches – following up all sorts of people who might have seen a ketch.'

Although there were points of tension between the police and private searchers – the public impression was that the families were searching because the police weren't doing a thorough enough job – there was some co-operation between them.

'There were some things that they could do through their private searches that would have taken a lot of organisation on our part, and which were not central to the needs of the inquiry,' John Rae says. 'They covered a lot of peripheral areas, like searching the shores of Queen Charlotte Sound. Had we had to organise that it would have taken a long time – we wouldn't have had the staff or the boats to do it, and it gave people the opportunity to contribute, show their support for the families. Gerald was a good organiser, and people did respond to his request for help.

'Often the police went back and covered some of those areas they had searched, not because we didn't think they had done it well but because there was some issue of interest there. Someone had recorded a bone washed up on a beach, or there was blood found in a hut – something like that – which we needed to go and check out for ourselves. I don't know how many caps they found that had blown off boaties, or ferries. But our exhibits officer went and collected everything from them and collated them all in case they were important.

'But generally they poured a lot of resources in, and we saw it as something which needed to be done that was additional to what we were doing. We were concentrating on certain areas, and it allowed us to get other things done.'

From the start, the volunteers of the Marlborough Coastguard played a crucial role in the search, ferrying police and other searchers – predominantly Air Force staff from the Woodbourne Base near Blenheim – out to the Sounds for each day's searching. The crews spent hours bucketing around the waterways of the Sounds in the Coastguard's two boats, the 6.8-metre *Tranz Rail* and the *Tranz Rail II*, a 12.6-metre Naiad which had originally seen service as an America's Cup chase boat – the one the Australian crew scrambled aboard when their boat split in two. At the height of the search about 75 personnel from Woodbourne were involved each day.

When the call went out for the Air Force to help with the search, Rob Pope found himself dealing with an old mate,

Squadron Leader Rob van Lent. They had played rugby together for Christchurch Boys' High School Old Boys back in the 1970s, so they immediately had a good rapport.

'When we came in, we were still looking for people, although the police had given us a warning that we may uncover some grotesque sights and we briefed our people about that,' van Lent says. 'The nature of the search changed over the days though, and it was soon pretty clear that we weren't searching for live people; we were now very much concentrating on finding evidence. At the time our feelings were still really hopeful that we were going to find these kids alive, or we were going to find something that indicated why they had disappeared so unexpectedly. But we were very conscious that we needed to have police input because none of our people were experienced in handling evidence. So my fear always was that in their haste to do something, our people might destroy something which the police might need to use later on.'

By the time the search was drawing to a close after more than six weeks of intensive work, police had paid about $30,000 for the Coastguard's fuel, oil and other costs – though they reckon they would have paid about $130,000 if they had used the commercial operators who were keen for the work and a bit resentful of the volunteers taking it from them.

'Most of them couldn't have done the work,' says Tony Groome, of the Coastguard. 'Not all of them could have spent 12 hours of the day, drop everything else. There was no way the police were going to pay those guys $400 or $500 an hour to sit around waiting. Because that's what they would have been wanting.'

Some of the Coastguard's volunteers had to abandon their day jobs for the search, and their bosses were happy to let them. It was something they could offer to support a case that all of Marlborough wanted to see solved. 'A lot of our guys knew the families involved, so that made it quite hard,' Groome says. 'Or they had kids who were down there for New Year, or were there themselves for that matter.'

Keen as they were, there was one aspect of the job that all the Coastguard volunteers came to hate. 'The media were, to put it mildly, a pain in the arse a lot of the time. One or two of our guys were getting to the stage where they were just about being followed by the media every time they went down to the vessel. There'd be a bloody reporter standing on the jetty checking to see where they were going, what they were up to. None of us were used to that, and it got bloody hard.'

The key Coastguard man was David Baker, a paua diver who knows the Sounds and its currents intimately, and who provided police with a lot of vital local knowledge. The main phase of the search coincided with some problems Baker was experiencing with the international marketing of paua, so he was happy to give his time.

'I skippered the boat for basically a whole month from about 3 January right through till early February. I was basically the main skipper, along with my son and a neighbour.'

Baker's diciest moments were dealing with the flotilla of craft that were helping with the private searches. 'I remember one day in particular when there was a fairly bad forecast and the boats really shouldn't have gone out. But no one had really liked to stop them. But then this southerly storm came up, and half of them didn't know what to do. You had the whole of Endeavour Inlet full of these little boats and a lot of them didn't have much experience. We could have had a real disaster on our hands. We were very lucky because it was a very severe blow, and a lot of them were panicking and didn't know what to do.' Baker directed the boats to the end of Endeavour Inlet, where they could see how bad it was out on Queen Charlotte Sound. If conditions were too bad, he intended to tell them all to go back and take shelter in Punga Cove. 'But we got to the outer end of Endeavour Inlet and it went flat calm. It was calm for about half an hour and then it blew like hell again, but that gave us enough time. So we were being looked after. After that I took on more of a role as marine co-ordinator.'

For weeks Baker ferried searchers out to Endeavour Inlet, and then beyond to Resolution Bay and Ship Cove, to go through the hard slog of searching the shoreline and bush tracks. 'It was very hard country to search. It was a prick of a thing to do, and unless they were extremely lucky the chance of finding anyone or anything was extremely unlikely. But if they didn't do it and somebody picked up something later, wouldn't they look stupid?

'Of course the poor families, they searched all the beaches. But as far as the police were concerned, they were concentrating on areas where the kids might have been taken ashore and had something horrible done to them. That could have been done. Police went to a few hot spots when they had tip-offs.'

In the end, all the searching came to nothing – or in Rob Pope's words, 'absolutely zip'.

'There was a lot of clothing and all sorts of paraphernalia that was located, but nothing that was attributable to the missing kids – not a thing,' he says. 'We had cavers, we had 75 Air Force staff help out, Search and Rescue staff, boaties, just a huge number of people. I take my hat off to the blokes. The actual area searched was just phenomenal. There were massive tracts of land that were searched very thoroughly.'

For Pope, it soon became apparent that the main focus of the searching would be 'exclusionary'. No evidence of value was likely to turn up, but the searching still had to continue so police could go to court and say they had ruled out all the possibilities.

'You had to put yourself in the defence mode. If we were to allege something, how could it be proved? If we hadn't carried out that extreme, intensive land search and immediate search in Endeavour Inlet, a lot of possibilities would have been left open. Could they have slipped overboard? They might be still on the bottom of the sea bed. No, that's fanciful. But the defence would have been able to say, "How do you know it's fanciful? You haven't checked." They could have gone up to the bushline for a midnight walk. So we had to search up there. All the scenarios which could be floated had to be negated. So we did a visual sea-bed search of Endeavour Inlet where all the boats were moored, and we located nothing on the sea bed. We did a land search from Punga Cove right round Endeavour Inlet to Furneaux Lodge and round past The Pines and out to the head.'

After weeks of work from hundreds of people, the searching had merely proved what *hadn't* happened.

Ben's and Olivia's parents were desperate enough to consider anything, and right now, after weeks of fruitless searching, a reward seemed like a good idea. Among themselves, they talked about offering cash to anyone who could come forward with some useful information. But police soon stymied the idea. They had a mountain of data to work through already, and it was growing fast. The prospect of being deluged by a whole lot more from cash-strapped cranks was too awful to contemplate.

7

TWO BOATS?

IT MAY NOT HAVE SEEMED that way at the time, but the weekend of 10–11 January was to be a turning point for Operation Tam. A number of leads were confirmed and some others dismissed. And police found themselves on strong enough ground to confront Scott Watson head-on about their suspicions. As Rob Pope put it later, by that weekend Watson was starting to 'stick out like dog's balls' as the prime suspect.

'We were now starting to get a lot of witnesses coming through. There were a few scuzzballs around but to all intents and purposes most of the people out there were quite reasonable sorts of blokes. There was talk of sleazy behaviour from some people, anti-social behaviour developing, not attributable to any particular individual. But we started to get this picture that Scott Watson had turned up, taken the kids on board and later disavowed any knowledge of them.'

During the weekend Wayne Stringer and his boat team were busy identifying more yachts and were getting close to accounting for every boat in Endeavour Inlet on New Year's Eve. Active inquiries were now under way with about 90 of the 100 boats identified, and Stringer expected to have run through all the identifiable boats by the following Monday.

Sightings of the publicised mystery ketch were coming in

from all around the country. One in particular, from Gisborne, attracted serious interest from police. A local woman was adamant she saw a boat exactly like the mystery ketch sailing out of Gisborne Harbour. Independently, another local who was unaware of the first woman's sighting reported to Gisborne police that he had seen a man who matched the compusketch. Like many other such sightings, it eventually drew a blank.

By the end of the weekend the Operation Tam team had approached the owners of at least 50 ketches that supposedly matched the description given by Guy Wallace. But they either didn't fit the bill or had clearly not been at Furneaux on the night. Some were not remotely similar to the mystery ketch. Another boat discounted was the *Mea New Zealand*, which was found to have been booked in at the Picton ferry terminal until 1 January.

The lack of any sighting of a ketch like the one described by Wallace was leading police to a difficult conclusion: that Wallace, their star witness, may have been mistaken. 'We can be fairly certain that this ketch does not exist but still cannot discount it completely,' Rob Pope told the daily briefing on Sunday.

Further, by that day, police had established that Watson's *Blade* had been moored very near the location Wallace said he had delivered the couple and the mystery man to on his last trip.

Still, the Operation Tam team was a way off going public with that change of stance. In the meantime it was working on plans to enhance one of the panoramic views of the inlet on New Year's Eve and have it published in newspapers in the hope that the handful of boats that had possibly escaped their inquiries might be recognised by someone in the public.

Over the weekend, police intensified their efforts to sort out Guy Wallace's evidence. Apart from his insistence on the ketch which they were beginning to doubt even existed, police were privately becoming concerned about a possible link between Wallace and Watson. As two young men in Picton, both interested in boats, it seemed hard to believe they didn't know each other. Wallace was talked to again but added nothing significant. He said he did know Scott Watson's mother, Beverley. About four years previously he had worked as a barman at the Beachcomber Motor Inn, in Picton, where Beverley worked in the kitchen. But he said he didn't know Scott Watson, and when shown a photo montage he did not pick him out. But police were not totally satisfied. They decided that Detective Tom Fitzgerald would put more work into establishing if there really was any local link between the water taxi driver and his passenger.

The doubts about Wallace's ketch put more focus back on Scott Watson and his yacht, the *Blade*. So did another troubling report received by police. A couple of kids had been playing with their toy walkie-talkies – no doubt Christmas presents – at Titirangi Bay in the northern the Marlborough Sounds on 2 January when they said they picked up a woman's voice putting out a may-day call. She said she was on a boat called the *Mad Dog*. At first police received only a second-hand report, but at the Operation Tam HQ they were particularly keen to check it out. Watson's *Blade* had previously been known by different names, including *Cascade*, *Caligula*, *Terror* and *Mad Dog*.

But at that point only a handful of people – mainly Watson's immediate family – could have known about the earlier name for the boat. There was no way the children with their walkie-talkies could have known they had stumbled into a major story with their talk of *Mad Dog*. And the source of their call remains unexplained.

'We've gone back to the manufacturers,' Rob Pope says. 'It was not possible under any atmospheric conditions for those radios to pick up marine radio. The other thing, the location of that bay, just does not equate. Watson could not have got around to that point and be back at Erie Bay at the time he was sighted there.

'That's going to be one of the odd mysteries.'

Police now faced a dilemma. The fragments of evidence they were gathering increasingly pointed to Scott Watson, especially if they could discount Guy Wallace's story of the ketch. But if they went to him now with their scenario, would that tip him off too soon and give Watson a chance to come up with explanations? Should they work at it for longer, and not approach him until they had a stronger case? On the other hand, their best bet for getting more evidence would be by seizing and examining Watson's boat, which they would do at the same time as talking to him. Over the weekend, the Operation Tam team came to the view that, despite the risks, they had a lot to gain by making their move now.

'The searches had located nothing,' Rob Pope later explained. 'We had to make a decision in relation to interviewing Watson. It was important that we get a much more detailed account of his movements than what he had previously provided, but it was also important that we lift the boat. But that was a real catch-22. Because we realised that as soon as we took that step there'd be no further chance of back-capturing any sort of information on Watson – he'd obviously know that we were looking at him far more closely.

'So it was very much a balancing act, in that we were only likely to get one bite of the cherry in terms of speaking to him. We'd have to lift the boat at the same time because at that stage we had no physical evidence. Would the boat actually yield us evidence or not? That was an unknown factor. We could have left the boat, but if there was anything else left on board, he would be bound to try to get rid of it after we'd talked to him, and we would lose evidence. But I thought we had no real option. It was a very carefully thought-out step to take. It was absolutely critical to how the inquiry was going to develop. If it wasn't Watson, who else were we going to have to look for? We had to eliminate him – or include him.'

Watson agreed to meet police at the Picton Police Station at noon on Monday 12 January. But when he didn't show, Detectives Tom Fitzgerald and Annie McCornick went to his parents' house. He was there with his mother Beverley, his sister Sandy, and her two young children.

Watson seemed nervous and agitated, and unwilling to go to the station. 'Why can't we do it here, mate?' he said to Fitzgerald. But he agreed to go, and by 12.45 p.m. he was back at the station where he spent about three hours giving Annie McCornick a statement.

Most of the time he stuck to the version of events he had already given police. But Pope said he stayed guarded throughout, especially over any involvement in the disappearance of Ben and Olivia. 'Then he just clammed up completely, shaking and looking quite emotional. He gave the detectives the impression on at least two or three occasions that he was just about to say something, and then just up go the shutters.'

He said he had sailed to Furneaux on the *Blade*, with a loose arrangement to meet a couple of friends there. 'Furneaux is, like, the place to be on New Year's Eve in the Sounds.' He arrived at about 2 p.m. after taking four or five hours to get from Waikawa Bay. The *Blade* was covered with weed underneath the waterline so made only about 3 knots speed. After he arrived he met up with some friends and spent the afternoon on their boat, the *Mina Cornelia*, 'sitting there getting pissed and watching all the boats come in'. He had a bottle of Captain Morgan rum, and drank at least half of it during the afternoon. After nightfall people started heading ashore and Watson said he went back to the *Blade*, had another drink and grabbed some clothes – jeans and 'a shirt or jersey . . . I think a grey one'.

Before he went ashore he ended up going back to the *Mina Cornelia*. That was when Scott Watson's evening seemed to turn sour. One thing that is utterly convincing in his account is the hazy image of a night recalled through a hangover.

'I started giving them all shit, like just talking with the guys. I think I took my rum, and smoked some drugs. It was dope. I had a couple of tokes. I don't know whose the dope was. It wasn't mine.

'I don't know what time I left. From this time on I was wasted.'

He said he didn't know how he got ashore. Maybe it was on a friend's inflatable, or maybe by water taxi.

'I don't know if I took my rum. I don't think I had any more left. I don't think I went up to the Lodge straight away. I don't know whether it was light or dark. Actually, I had something else as well to drink. I had a couple of other things by that stage and I was pretty written off.

'I was wasted. It was New Year's. I don't remember what kind of mood I was in. I was in a good mood.'

But he did remember getting involved in some aggro throughout the evening.

'The next thing I remember was some guy saying I had spilt my drink. I was in the back of the bar. There are double doors with glass in them . . . There was a whole bunch of bikies there. I was calling them a bunch of loose cunts. I was shit-stirring. Actually, I wouldn't have been arguing. I would have been having them on.'

In fact, he said, he didn't remember saying that to the bikies, but a friend had told another guy that that's what he had been doing. But Watson recalled other glimpses of the evening.

'There was a woman having a shit on the end of the wharf. I can't remember what she looked like. I think this was on the

Ben – friendly, trusting and keen on a good night out.

Olivia wearing the greenstone pendant her father gave her for Christmas 1997.

Against the darkening skyline, was it possible to count masts and distinguish sloops from ketches?

The police's aerial view of the jetty and foreshore at Furneaux Lodge where Ben and Olivia spent most of the evening.

Olivia and her friends sailed to Furneaux from Picton on a chartered yacht, the *Tamarack*.

One of Furneaux's water taxis took Ben and Olivia on their last voyage to Scott Watson's *Blade*, police argued.

Ben and Olivia walked down the track to the jetty at Furneaux Lodge in the early hours of New Year's morning and were never seen on land again.

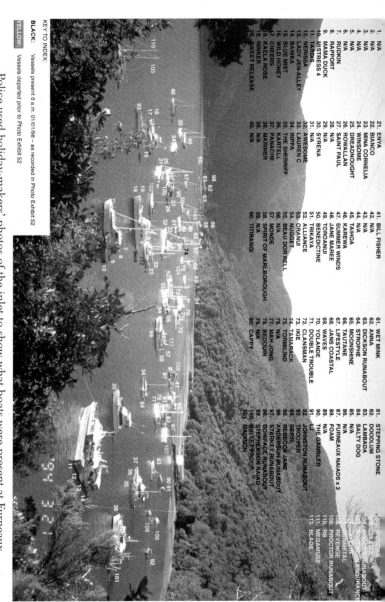

Police used holiday-makers' photos of the inlet to show what boats were present at Furneaux on New Year's morning – and where they were moored.

BEFORE

The *Blade*, before and after its blue New Year's Day paint job,
which Watson did at Erie Bay.

AFTER

The police shot of Scott Watson, prime suspect.

Scott Watson was pictured at about 10 p.m. on New Year's Eve. The photo caused an uproar at the depositions when Guy Wallace said Watson seemed too clean-shaven to have been the stranger he ferried to a boat later that night. The clothes Watson was wearing in this photograph have never been found.

Police seized the *Blade* and hauled it out
of the water for forensic examination.

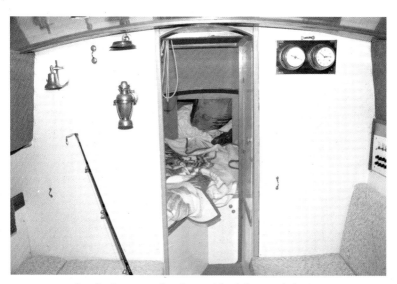

Inside the meticulously scrubbed-down *Blade*, the
door is open to the area where Watson slept.

The police's enhanced photo of the inside of the *Blade*'s hatch cover, immediately above the bed, shows 176 scratch marks – the product of an attack or a frenzied attempt to escape?

A patch of foam has been cut from one of the swabs inside the *Blade*. Police argued that Watson may have been trying to remove blood stains.

main part of the wharf. I'm not sure if anyone else was there. I don't know. Somehow I was down there. That was before midnight.

'I can remember midnight. I was outside the beer tent thing, I think. Someone yelled out that it was 12 o'clock.

'I remember talking to some people in the bar, having an argument with him about him wearing a pearl necklace. He got upset 'cause he reckoned his sister gave it to him and she was dead or something. He might have had his girlfriend or his friends there. It was a beaded pearl necklace like women wear. He got all fuckin' upset about me giving him a hard time.'

Did he put the hard word on any women? 'I probably was chatting up some women. I can't remember. Probably.'

Then Watson recalled fragments of his return to the *Blade*. 'I can remember getting on my boat. I remember the guy saying to me not to get into the taxi from the wharf. I don't know what he was up to. I think he was making it safe for me to get off the wharf onto the Naiad.

'I think he had a hat on, a cap. I think he was old. I had seen him earlier on that afternoon whizzing around dropping people off, picking them up. I'm not sure whether I got a lift in with him or not. I had no trouble getting off the Naiad onto my boat.

'I think it was about 2 a.m. I have got a feeling it was about then. I'm not exactly sure. I don't think I had a sleep or anything like that because if I had I would have still been there the next day.

'I went out alone to my boat. There was only myself and the Naiad driver. I got onto my boat first, then I think I jumped straight onto the *Mina Cornelia* and woke them up. I don't know who I spoke to. It was a guy that way laying there in his bunk. I couldn't see his face. I said to him to get out of bed. I wondered why they had all gone to sleep. The boat would have been full of people, but it was dark so I couldn't see. I don't know.

'So I went back to my boat and had something to eat 'cause I was hungry. Then I went to bed.'

As well as being a bit confused over whether he went to bed or not, Watson also suggested that he may have hopped onto another of the boats rafted up with the *Blade* and the *Mina Cornelia*. But they too were all asleep, and he returned to the *Blade* without saying anything to them. From his account, his big night out had hardly ended well. He had started out boozing and chatting up girls, but ended it alone, pestering anyone he could find for a bit more fun. But he said he wasted no time getting moving on New Year's morning.

'After waking up, I checked the oil in the motor and left. It was about half-past 6, 7 o'clock when I left. It was dawn anyway. It was daylight. I'm guessing it was that time. It was early but it was a nice day.

'The neighbours weren't up and about. I didn't see anyone else. I untied my boat and left. I headed down to Tory Channel, to Erie Bay. I had a hangover, but I wasn't sick. I'd had a feed and heaps of water before I went to bed.'

On his way out of Endeavour Inlet, Watson said he saw a small cruise boat fishing near Marine Head. He said he arrived at Erie Bay about 9.30 a.m. or 10 a.m., moored at the wharf and went to see a friend. He said he stayed at the friend's place for three days before returning to Shakespeare Bay, near Picton, where he normally moored the *Blade*. He went straight to his parents' house, where his brother was visiting with his wife and kids. They all went out for tea at the Toot 'n' Whistle. Watson said the Toot 'n' Whistle was one of his drinking holes, along with the Terminus and the Federal.

He ended his statement with some curt replies to McCornick's questions.

He hadn't heard any screaming or shouting when he went to bed.

He didn't remember seeing Ben Smart or Olivia Hope.

He didn't see the ketch while he was at Furneaux. There was a ketch there, but it wasn't the same as the description.

He said he didn't know Guy Wallace. But he had read in the paper that he was a water taxi driver at Furneaux.

He didn't remember telling anyone about thoughts of going on a trip to Tonga.

He didn't recall seeing anything strange while he was at Furneaux.

He couldn't think of anything else that could help.

It was now after 4 p.m. It had been a long interview. But Watson's time with the police wasn't finished. Tom Fitzgerald wanted to discuss the statement with him, but Watson was having doubts about whether he should sign it. He worried it might make him look bad.

If it was true, why wouldn't he want to sign it? Fitzgerald asked.

'Yeah, it's true, mate,' Watson told him, and he signed the statement.

Fitzgerald wanted to know if he was certain about what he had been wearing that night.

'Yeah, a tee-shirt and a grey jersey,' he said.

What about his attitude towards women that night? He had apparently been rude and aggressive, and Fitzgerald wanted to know if that was normal for him.

'I was just trying to score,' Watson said. 'What's wrong with that? It was New Year's Eve.'

Fitzgerald then went through Watson's denial of ever having seen Ben and Olivia. Watson said he would certainly remember if he had talked to Olivia because she was an attractive girl.

What about his account of being taken out to the *Blade* alone on a Naiad by an old guy with a cap on? Fitzgerald said to him the Naiad drivers had been so busy that night they hadn't taken any single passengers but had waited until there was a group wanting to go.

'Look, mate, I've made a fucking statement,' Watson shouted back.

On his timings, he said he was sure he had returned to the Blade at about 2 a.m.; and he stuck to the 6.30 a.m. to 7 a.m. timing of his departure, even though Fitzgerald told him that some people said his boat had been gone from the inlet by 6 a.m.

When Fitzgerald put it to him that he knew Guy Wallace, Watson denied it, saying he had no idea who Fitzgerald was talking about.

Then Fitzgerald got to his main point: he told Watson he believed he knew Ben and Olivia, and that he had had them on his boat on New Year's morning.

'I've told you, I've never seen them before,' Watson said. 'You'll find who did it, mate. I've got nothing to do with it. I've never fucking seen them before.'

Watson had another, more intriguing comment to make about the young couple's fate. 'They'll turn up on the 16th,' he said. When asked why he believed that, Watson said they had to start work. He couldn't give a valid reason for why he made the comment.

Fitzgerald summed up Watson's mood as rude and aggressive – and evasive. 'When questions were put to him he constantly looked away and would not make eye contact with me.'

As Rob Pope came to see it, that interview with Watson on 12 January gave the investigation 'the most critical bit of information we have'. It was not merely what he told them that mattered, but the crucial points in his narrative that, even at that early stage, they knew from other witnesses to be lies. 'So really our course was set from that day.'

Watson's description of his clothing that night was one of the key 'rebuttables' for Pope. 'What we do know is that at no stage was he wearing that grey jersey with red stripes. Witnesses, and photographs, show him wearing a blue denim shirt.

'None of the clothing Watson was wearing on the evening has ever been found, apart from a pair of Bianchi sportshoes that Watson was apparently wearing on the night and was still wearing later when we talked to him. Other witnesses said he was wearing brown leather shoes that night, but we never resolved that claim. He told us we'd find the clothing on the boat, but we didn't. Nor have any of Ben's or Olivia's clothing or possessions been found.

'We know he got into Wallace's water taxi at about 4 a.m. And we know that at 5 a.m. or just thereafter he slipped his moorings and left the inlet, and that he arrived at Erie Bay sometime after 5 p.m. on New Year's Day.

'What we worked out is that over the period of time from when he was grogging up on the boat and smoking a bit of cannabis, his behaviour deteriorated over the evening. He was involved in a number of incidents over the course of the evening at Furneaux, where he was either aggressive verbally or resorted to sexual innuendo, offering Prozac for sex and hitting on several women during the evening.

'Of critical importance is that during the evening he spent a considerable amount of time – like an hour and a half or so – propped on the end of the bar at a place called Reg's Corner. They had two cash registers operating on the evening, and Watson was sitting at the bar making a nuisance of himself. Both Wallace and a woman, Ros McNeilly, who was the bar manageress, commented on how annoyed they were at this bloke who kept getting in the way, ordering double bourbons. The importance of that is that Ros McNeilly identified Watson from a photographic montage, saying that is the bloke who was at the bar who made a real nuisance of himself.

'And Wallace said the bloke he dropped off at the ketch, the unidentified male, is the same bloke that made a nuisance of himself in the bar, sitting there ordering bourbons. He was a constant nuisance. When he was ultimately shown the photographic montage he said that was the person he dropped off with the two kids. And that's corroborated thankfully by this Ros McNeilly – because of the difficulties we had with Wallace and his media attention.'

While Watson was being interviewed, other police were searching his parents' house in Picton. They found little of note. There were a lot of papers, and two cameras which they took to see if their films might show anything. But there was nothing of interest.

Meanwhile, in Shakespeare Bay, another police team was carrying out the third part of the calculated sting operation on Scott Watson – seizing his boat for investigation. Their action provided Operation Tam with its biggest media event to date. Police were concerned about protecting whatever potentially valuable forensic evidence the *Blade* might hold; David Baker, a volunteer with the Marlborough Coastguard, was the skipper of the vessel that was charged with seizing the *Blade*, and he had more practical worries on his mind – and a big media contingent watching every move as he towed the boat into the Picton marina.

'This thing was not easy to keep steering,' Baker says. 'I thought, If I cock up today it's not going to be a good day. Of course, we weren't allowed to touch the vessel.'

To control the *Blade* while it was being attached and towed from Shakespeare Bay, it would have been normal boaties' practice to have somebody on board, but police didn't want any evidence tampered with. So the job had to be done without any effective control over the *Blade*.

'It wouldn't tow. We just put it on a long line and did our best. We also didn't know what might be on board, so it was a fairly dramatic moment. I said to the forensic guy from the cops that I hoped like hell we'd got the right boat, because if we didn't, all the news media were here and they'd soon tell.'

In the tight Sounds boaties' community, Baker also had a few concerns about being too closely identified with the police operation which was now effectively targeting one of the boaties themselves. 'If in fact this wasn't the right person's boat, the Coastguard were assisting with it, which sort of branded us in a sense. I was trying to keep as low a profile as I could, so I put on my sunglasses. I didn't mind helping, but I didn't want to be seen too much. I was just doing it because I had the time to spare and I wanted to help, basically.'

To make matters more difficult, when Baker towed the *Blade* into the marina, he found the place packed with yachts from the Heineken regatta which had just been held. It was difficult finding room to manoeuvre the boat. Once he had a chance to have a look over the *Blade*, however, his first impressions were positive. 'I thought it was a reasonable little craft. It was a home-built boat and as far as home-built boats go, it was moderately professional. It was quite sturdy. Yeah, it was a tidy enough little ship.'

The *Blade* was taken immediately to a hangar at Woodbourne Air Base. Forensic scientists from the Institute of Environmental Science and Research (ESR) had a preliminary look at the outside of the *Blade* but found nothing of note. There was one point that could be significant, though. The *Blade* had had a blue paint job since New Year's Day. Watson hadn't been asked to explain that, and police were clearly going to be very interested in whatever explanation he came up with.

But Pope, meanwhile, was trying to hose down media speculation that the seizure of the *Blade* was a significant development for the case. Asked at his daily press conference if the taking of the boat was a breakthrough for Operation Tam, Pope said, 'Certainly not.' He refused to comment on whether the boat fitted the description of the ketch. And he said nobody was in custody; nor were police looking for anybody.

The Tam investigators now had to get down to the laborious work of scouring the *Blade* from end to end in search of possible forensic evidence. At the same time, the Smart and Hope families were beginning their own more difficult task – confronting the possibility that Ben and Olivia might be permanently gone. Detective Dick Rolton noted that night that the families 'seemed resigned to the fact that their children will not be coming back'.

Police, too, were becoming resigned to a difficult fact for their own inquiry – that the ketch perhaps did not exist.

In his evening briefing on Wednesday 14 January, Rob Pope told the Operation Tam staff that the decision had been made to announce publicly that the inquiry had shifted its focus from the ketch to Watson's boat. Admitting that the ketch had been a red herring would be a major public relations hurdle, but they would just have to confront it.

'We will leave the door open in terms of ketch sightings, but essentially the public will be told that despite extensive inquiries and saturation of boat owners and occupants, we have yet to identify this ketch,' Pope said. The plan would be to issue a press release that put the emphasis on the *Blade*, along with before-and-after photographs showing the paint job Watson had done on the boat immediately after New Year. The intention was to increase the pressure on Watson to see what new information would turn up, both from Watson and his family, and from members of the public whose memories might be jogged by the new information.

Pope told the briefing that already they had compiled an outline of Watson's movements. That included a visit with his sister Sandy to the Picton Supervalue supermarket on the morning of New Year's Eve – and police were talking to the supermarket management to see if his visit had been recorded on the supermarket's security video. At some stage he had sailed on the *Blade* to Endeavour Inlet and moored up alone at about 7.30 p.m. A bit later, he went ashore and 'made a complete fool of himself within the Furneaux Lodge area during the evening – sleazing around women, offering sex for a tee-shirt, etc'. According to his own account he had returned to the *Blade* at around 2 a.m., had a sleep and set off for Erie Bay at about 7 a.m. Other witnesses had given police different accounts – including that he had got on board the *Mina Cornelia* and the *Bianco* between 4 a.m. and 5 a.m. and hassled the crews, and that photographic evidence showed he had left the Inlet by 6 a.m. There was also a report from a nearby boat of a female voice coming from the direction of the *Blade* sometime in the early dawn.

The press release that marked a major turning point in Operation Tam went out at 8 p.m. on Wednesday 14 January: 'Police Unable to Locate Ketch.' Inquiries so far had been unable to locate anyone who verified the existence of the ketch, Pope said. 'This does not, however, mean that the ketch does not exist . . . and he [Detective Inspector Pope] is still interested in hearing from anybody who saw a similar boat in the Sounds over this period.' But then Pope shifted focus to Watson's boat.

'The boat which has been seized by police was in Endeavour Inlet over New Year's Eve. Its owner has similarities to the unidentified person last seen by the water taxi driver with Olivia and Ben. Inquiries are focused on eliminating or otherwise this boat being involved in the disappearance of Olivia and Ben.

'Detective Inspector Pope says that this is a line of inquiry which needs to be pursued. He asks that anyone who saw the boat contact the operation base. It is believed that the boat has been repainted some time during the first week of January. On 31 December 1997 it is described as having a white hull, reddy-brown superstructure, solar panel, single mast, wind vane, towing a ply dinghy. The boat was seized on Monday afternoon. It now has a dark blue trim and superstructure. Police are seeking any information as to the movements of this vessel. The boat is in the process of being searched with the assistance of forensic expertise.'

Pope then continued with an update of the inquiry. 'The search around the baches in Endeavour Inlet will commence tomorrow. However, owners should be assured that staff will not enter properties unless there is an owner or representative present or there is evidence that the bach has been tampered with or entered illegally. Mr Pope says that there are about 60 baches to check and it may take longer than one day. Nothing of any significance has been found from the ground searches at this stage.

'A search has been conducted of the Erie Bay area today where it is known that the boat which the police have seized was moored on 1 January 1998. I want to emphasise that this is a private property and in no way is the owner under any suspicion whatsoever. The owner has been extremely co-operative with police.'

Watson's New Year's Day visit to Erie Bay was to become a fundamental part of the police case – but it was also difficult for police to pin down, because of confusion and inconsistencies among different accounts of the timings of the visit.

Detective Sergeant Dave Harvey had travelled out to the isolated Erie Bay that day to follow up Watson's own story that he sailed there on New Year's Day. He had found that the 168- hectare property there was owned by a man from out of the Sounds whose name has been suppressed. He had inter-mittently employed Watson as a sort of odd-jobs man over the last three years. The man did not live on the property in Tory Channel but had a caretaker living there. The caretaker lived in the house at Erie Bay rent-free in return for looking after the place. The caretaker told Harvey that he noticed the *Blade* in the bay some time on New Year's morning (in later interviews, the caretaker confirmed that Watson had in fact arrived after 5 p.m.). Later, Watson came ashore and 'mucked about' for a while on the property. At some stage Watson had cut his foot on a piece of glass on the beach. He said Watson had stayed on the yacht until the next morning, when he set off in the direction of Picton.

The caretaker gave Harvey the impression he didn't know Watson very well but, intriguingly, he said Watson had phoned him twice in the past few days and told him to expect a visit from the police. Harvey also discovered that Watson had earlier bought some dark blue paint from the Erie Bay property, saying he wanted to paint his boat. And the caretaker's daughter recalled the *Blade* as being blue, whereas it had been a reddy-brown colour before New Year. Overall, Harvey didn't think he had got much out of the guy.

But police did find something they hadn't been looking for.

'He kept asking, "What are those blokes looking for?"' Pope said. '"Where are they going?" the caretaker asked. "How far are they going up there?" We said, "Oh, have you got something up there?" "I might have a bit of personal stuff," he said. And we had a fair idea what he was talking about. "Oh yeah, how much?" "Not much." The sweat's starting to pour from him. And we came across about 200 marijuana plants. "Oh, you bastards," he said. It ruined his cash crop for the year and he was really pissed off about it. It was quite funny really.'

Later, there were suggestions around Marlborough that police had turned a blind eye to the crop in return for the caretaker's co-operation in the inquiry. In fact, he was charged with possession for supply. He pleaded guilty and was given a two-year suspended sentence.

It would take police some time to establish all the details about Watson's visit to Erie Bay. They were most interested in two things: precisely when he arrived, and the unexplained time that gave him after leaving Endeavour Inlet to have possibly disposed of the bodies; and what he did while moored at Erie Bay, such as repainting the *Blade* and cleaning it up to get rid of evidence.

If indeed the *Blade*, not the mystery ketch, was the boat they were after, police were having a hard time finding much evidence on board. Out at the Woodbourne Air Base, police were giving the *Blade* a full forensic search. So far they had found two definite blood spots inside the cabin – one in the main cabin and the other on the toilet door. There also appeared to be blood stains or smears on a blanket on Watson's bed. But the luminol testing for body fluids being carried out on all the fittings inside the cabin had not shown up much of evidential significance. To establish whether the blood stains were from Watson himself, or from Ben or Olivia, police first needed a sample from Watson. When they asked him for a sample on Wednesday 14 January he at first refused. But after a mate apparently told him that if he was sure he was innocent he should oblige, Watson changed his mind and let police take a thumb-prick sample. Police said he had a 'cocky' attitude when they took the blood.

But it was becoming apparent that the most significant evidence on the *Blade* may have been what was *not* present, rather than what was. None of Ben's or Olivia's clothing or other possessions were on the boat – nor were they found anywhere else. Nor was the clothing Watson had been wearing on New Year's Eve. 'Our immediate observation of the boat was that it had been very, very thoroughly cleaned down in specific areas,' Rob Pope says. 'Any surface that was likely to have fingerprints on it had been wiped down, even to the extent of underneath any benches. The GPS system and the radio had been removed from their brackets and cleaned behind. There were 58 cassette tapes and covers, and each of them had been individually cleaned and wiped down. But in other areas, like the kitchen and galley area, it was quite dirty. It was full of dirty pots and pans. So Watson was hardly house-proud on the *Blade*, but for some reason he had gone to a lot of trouble to clean part of it.'

The sweep of the cabin was finding some other factors that could be important, too. Holes had been cut in the cover of a squab in the cabin, and police wondered if that had been done to remove blood stains. And the rubber lining of a hatch built into the ceiling of the cabin immediately above the bed was very badly scratched. Police sent it to the Institute of Environmental Science and Research (ESR) to see if the forensic scientists there could establish what had caused the scratching. They reported back that there were 176 multi-directional scratches which appeared to have been made by fingernails rather than any instrument. They were to put months of work into trying to extract any DNA samples from the scratch marks, to see who had made them.

Most of all, the police wanted to see if there was any forensic evidence on the *Blade* which could prove that Ben and Olivia had been on board. That would give huge weight to their view that this must be the boat that Guy Wallace had delivered Watson and the couple to, and help dismiss Wallace's theory of a ketch. About 1300 hairs and fibres were removed from various parts of the boat. Most were irrelevant, but about 400 from a tiger-print blanket directly beneath the hatch cover were possibly vital so they were passed on to the ESR for examination. Most of them proved to be insignificant. But some three and a half months into the inquiry, the ESR called Pope and said that going purely by hair colour and type, six hair samples may be significant. Two hair strands had been found on the tiger-print blanket, and four more were found in the bristles of a scrubbing brush on board. They gave a reasonably compatible match with samples of Olivia Hope's hair that had been collected from her bedroom. However, just one had a root follicle attached, which the ESR scientists felt might be able to deliver a DNA sample.

'They did a blood screening DNA test which came up with a result of a 1 in 500 probability that it was Olivia Hope's hair rather than anyone else's, which wasn't fantastic,' Pope says. 'They then said there was a very small amount of DNA left that they wanted to submit to a much more sophisticated process called SGM, which is more discriminatory. They ran that and came up with a negative result. The sample was too small and they just couldn't get it to register.'

Pope was getting increasingly frustrated about the prospect of the ESR's DNA testing coming up with anything useful.

At that point Pope and Detective Paul Merrett went up to the ESR and had a bit of a session. 'We said, "What is it that we really need to do? What tests are available, not in New Zealand but overseas?" So we sat down and worked out a regime that had this very small amount of DNA which we could have run through this SGM technique, but then it would have been destroyed forever. Each time you do it, it diminishes the sample. They said there was another test which they were hopeful of replicating the 1 in 500 – a test in Sydney called the DQ Alpha test. They are very experienced in dealing with minute amounts of DNA.

'We discussed at length the other hairs that didn't have follicles. I wondered if there was anything we could do with the DNA in the hair shafts themselves.' The ESR said there were two laboratories in the world – Forensic Science Services in London, attached to the Home Office, and an American laboratory – that do what is called Mitochondrial DNA testing, or MDNA, which works by testing a different part of the DNA's protein chain to that done by the ESR.

'I decided we'd hang fire on that at this stage but send a sample to Sydney for the DQ Alpha test.' The result came back eventually, and, combined with other tests, pointed to a 1 in 28,000 probability that it was Olivia's hair rather than anyone else's. 'That was much more positive. We felt it was sufficient for us to proceed with charging Watson.'

While waiting for that result, Pope had decided to try the MDNA technique at Forensic Science Services in London. He sent that laboratory three of the four hairs from the scrubbing brush and two from the tiger blanket. The results did not come back until late 1998. One hair showed a positive match with Olivia's. The others came back with a mixed profile – the result for the DNA in the hair shaft had been contaminated with DNA from another source, possibly semen, saliva or blood. The laboratory set about attempting to wash the fluid off the shaft and run the hair sample again. Pope was in for a long wait for anything conclusive from that hair. Eventually, the London laboratory discounted two of the hairs from the brush as Olivia's and said one was likely to be hers. And that was the strand that the physical evidence side of Pope's case came to hang on.

'Yes that's it. That's the case. But Watson had had eight days really to do all the cleaning up.'

As for the forensic case against Watson himself, Pope readily admitted there were fish hooks. 'He could say he just brushed up beside her at Furneaux Lodge during the evening and the hairs just happened to be transferred. That's where Wallace's evidence is critical in actually putting the pair on the boat.'

The problem there, though, was that Wallace was claiming he put them on a different boat – the still unfound ketch.

And they had another problem: Watson was on the move. In late February they had a call from his ex-girlfriend. Watson had turned up unexpectedly at her place in Whangarei. She said she just didn't know what to do and had agreed to let him stay there. She said she wanted to come down to Marlborough to have a look at the *Blade*, but Watson was telling her not to have anything to do with the police. She didn't think she could come down while he was staying at her place. But she agreed to keep in touch with Operation Tam.

8

STAR WITNESS

F ROM THE START, GUY WALLACE had been Operation Tam's
star witness. As the last witness to have seen Ben and Olivia
alive, and the water taxi driver who delivered them to what
they believed was Scott Watson's boat, he was the vital link in
the police's chain of evidence. But he was a witness who posed
the police a few problems, quite apart from his insistence that
he delivered the pair to a ketch. There were questions over his
identification of Watson: his description of the mystery man he
had taken on board his taxi differed from other descriptions of
Watson on New Year's Eve. But he had identified the mystery
man and the man at the bar as the same. Then there were the
lingering worries over possible connections between Wallace
and Watson. There were public rumours that the two were
somehow co-operating to confuse the police. That was probably
mere gossip, but police had to discount the possibility. Then
there was Wallace's relations with the media. To the police, he
seemed all too willing to court the media, relishing his time in
the limelight and offering reporters detailed accounts of what he
had seen and done that night. This was a witness who enjoyed
being a star. It all meant the police had their work cut out if they
were one day to deliver him to court as a vital witness in their
case against Scott Watson.

Privately, some police grumbled that Wallace was altogether too sure of himself. They also feared that, despite his cockiness, the strain of all the media attention he had invited was beginning to show on him.

By the middle of January it looked as if the police had good grounds to worry on several fronts. On Monday 19 January TVNZ ran a story claiming that Wallace was a regular at the same Picton hotel as Watson. Wallace, for one, decided that he had had enough of TVNZ. The next day he went to the Blenheim Police Station and asked how he could take out a trespass notice against TVNZ staff. He told police he was particularly pissed off with the reporter TVNZ had covering the case, Julie Roberts. He said she was continually visiting his parents. They were getting rattled by the whole thing, and Wallace wanted to put an end to it. He said he was quite happy to talk to TV3 because they were all right, but he wanted nothing more to do with *One Network News*. Police gave him some trespass notices and told him not to discuss the matter with the media. If reporters visited his property, he could ask them to leave. At least Wallace was continuing to co-operate. He told police that he had bought a ticket to fly to Cairns on 14 February, for work on the prawn boats. But he had decided to cancel his flight because he realised the inquiry was going to be a long, drawn-out affair.

Meanwhile, police were trying to ascertain if there was any connection between Wallace and Watson, going back to when they were boys. Like Watson, Guy Wallace had moved about frequently as a child. But the list of schools they got from Wallace – St George's in Invercargill, Edgecumbe Primary, Apanui Primary in Whakatane, Gisborne Boys' High and Whakatane High School – showed that at least they had never sat in a classroom together.

But there was plenty more to worry about. A couple of weeks after Wallace approached police about taking out a trespass order against Julie Roberts, Detective Tom Fitzgerald went to see him at his work at Punga Cove for another interview, and Wallace told Fitzgerald that Julie Roberts had also been out and had showed him a videotape of a person she believed was Watson. Wallace said he had looked at the tape and told the reporter that the man was not the person he had taken to the yacht with Ben and Olivia. Fitzgerald warned Wallace of the dangers of making that sort of identification, and said it was vital for any witness involved with the inquiry to follow the right procedures to avoid jeopardising the reliability of anything they might later say in court.

Wallace was then called away from his talk with Fitzgerald to help unload passengers and baggage from the Cougar Line water taxi. When he came back, he had changed his story.

'I have just rung Julie Roberts from TVNZ and told her I didn't want her to show that story,' he told Fitzgerald. 'I've thought about it and I don't think I can stand by what I said.' Fitzgerald told Wallace he was free to speak to whoever he liked, but he should remember the procedures he would have to follow as a witness.

TVNZ went ahead with the item, adding to the growing list of gripes Pope was building against the media. The story centred on local disquiet at the direction Operation Tam was taking, and in particular the inquiry's focus on Scott Watson and his sloop. It featured three people who had given statements to police, all of whom suggested that the police were concentrating on the wrong man and the wrong boat. They said police should be seeking another man, whom they said had been seen both at Furneaux Lodge and on the water taxi during Ben's and Olivia's last recorded ride. One witness described the man acting 'sleazily' at the New Year's party, while Wallace said that it was this man who offered Olivia and Ben a berth on his yacht. They also remained adamant that the water taxi dropped Olivia and Ben at a ketch, rather than Scott Watson's smaller sloop.

Two witnesses who described the 'mystery man' were shown pictures of Scott Watson, and both said categorically that he was not the man they had seen.

For weeks, Pope had thought the media were going too far. Instead of merely reporting developments as police released them, he felt reporters were trying to run the case themselves. His big worry now was that the TVNZ report would jeopardise any subsequent trial. Identification of Watson was clearly going to be crucial at the trial, and television's story would undermine the credibility of the witnesses he was hoping to use to identify Watson as the man at the centre of the case. The attempts at identification used by TVNZ were totally at odds with the strict requirements police have to meet for identification to be admissible in court. TVNZ's identification was unfair, unreasonable, and stood every chance of 'tainting' witness testimony to the point where it would have been dangerous or impossible to call witnesses to give evidence.

Pope believed that by broadcasting the story, TVNZ was in contempt of court. But when he sought legal advice, he was told there was little police could do. Discomforting and unhelpful as the story may have been, it didn't amount to contempt of court because there were as yet no proceedings under way against Watson. Tactically, police would be on dubious grounds if they tried to pursue a contempt charge. Inevitably, the media would depict such action as an attempt by police to close down criticisms and unhelpful views such as people coming forward supporting the ketch theory. At least until there was an arrest, police would just have to put up with a lot of adverse publicity.

Dealing with the media was always a balancing act for Pope. He needed to give reporters enough to generate publicity that might help with the case, while trying to keep them from going off on angles of their own that he thought were distinctly unhelpful.

But in late January Operation Tam found itself in the centre of a media storm that was entirely of its own making. Early in the month the team analyst, Mike Porter, had compiled victim profiles of Ben Smart and Olivia Hope that attempted to look dispassionately at the two. The profiles were standard police procedure; by knowing more about the pair, it was possible that police may discover some aspect of their characters or their behaviour that could have played a part in their disappearance. And by showing the profiles to the right people, maybe they would trigger some new information. But somehow the profiles went far further. In an attempt to reach boaties, the profiles were distributed around yacht clubs up and down the country, including at least two in Auckland, and some of the clubs put them on their notice boards. Inevitably, reporters quickly heard about them, and some newspapers, led by the *New Zealand Herald* in Auckland, decided to publish what they had found.

Readers of the *Herald*, and other papers that decided to run at least parts of the profile, found out that police had assessed Olivia as spoiled, emotional, close to her mother, sexually active and fond of a drink. Ben was described as fun-loving, easy-going, sociable and popular.

Gerald Hope immediately demanded a meeting with Pope and complained loudly to the media at what he saw as a slur on his missing daughter's character. 'I am absolutely staggered the police are saying this about our daughter. It is gross mis-representation, completely irrelevant and will greatly hinder the police inquiry,' he told reporters.

Pope, too, was furious that the memos had found their way to the media and that some outlets, at least, had been 'irresponsible' enough to publish excerpts. He apologised to the families and described the incident as a 'leak'. He also launched an internal inquiry into how the memos had been made public. 'This is confidential police information which certainly should not be in the hands of boat clubs or the media,' he said. He accused the papers of being 'unthinking and callous' and said they had brought 'unnecessary distress' to Ben's and Olivia's families by deciding to publish the information.

The publications that had decided to run the reports were indignant that they, not the police, were being fingered. Some pointed out that they had self-censored some of the more 'brutal' comments, and were quick to justify why they had published what they did. Wellington's *Evening Post*, for instance, said the 'monumental mistake' exposed not merely a bungle by the police but some outdated attitudes as well.

'Let's be generous here,' the *Post* wrote in an editorial. 'Most can accept the police team tracking the missing pair must be weary. It's already been a three-week job during which they have interviewed literally thousands of people, spent long hours securing evidence and searching difficult terrain, and withstood rumour, speculation and criticism from those inside and outside Marlborough for their often confused and taciturn public statements. It should be accepted too that hurtful as it may be, they are obliged to draw up a complete picture of any victim of crime if it will help solve it. Frank as the assessments of Olivia Hope and Ben Smart might be – and much as they may pain Olivia's parents – this is part of dogged and thorough police work.

'Two points stand out, however. First, these summaries should never have been made available to the public. Assistant Police Commissioner Ian Holyoake, trying to mend fences, has already conceded that. Second, however – and more important – is the double standard the police have employed in describing the young people at the heart of this inquiry. Why should Olivia be described in pejorative terms as emotional, sexually active and a drinker, when Ben is referred to as a 'social type'? Isn't the latter description a kinder way of saying the same thing as said of Olivia Hope?

'Why, in 1998, is it still OK for young men to sow their wild oats, to have a sex life and to enjoy alcohol – getting drunk is almost a male rite of passage – but for young women who similarly enjoy life to be still frowned upon? Few parents would admit it but most know privately that their teenage children and those in their 20s have sex, drink alcohol, have probably suffered a hangover, may have smoked dope, and are still, in some cases, fond of their families. The description of Olivia Hope could apply equally to literally thousands of young New Zealanders. The female variety should not be forced to carry a stigma that does not attach to their male counterparts. The police need more women in their ranks who understand that.'

In Hamilton, the *Waikato Times* was similarly indignant in justifying why it had decided to publish reports of the profiles. 'The press are not the culprits here. The police wrote the profiles and released them. It was their error. The press reported that. This newspaper has chosen to publish the full profiles of the missing pair rather than titillate its readers about what was really said.

'What was said, in fact, was not shocking. Young people do have sex and drink. What was astounding was that only Olivia was said to indulge in both. The implication is that Olivia was not behaving properly. Young women, apparently, still aren't supposed to do those things. Did Ben not have a sex life? Was he a non-drinker? Wasn't he emotional? And, if so, is that such an awful thing?

'Attitudes towards men and women have moved some distance in the past two decades. But some things haven't changed. Young women who have sex are still cheap; young men are studs. Young women who drink alcohol are irresponsible; young men fun-loving, party animals. Women are emotional (read irrational and flighty).

'Olivia Hope did what most young women do at her age: have a social life. The comments in her police profile could be made of almost any young person – male or female. Any parent will attest to that. She has done nothing wrong. From all accounts she is a loving daughter, sister and friend.

'She does not deserve to be the subject of innuendo and salacious gossip because of a police blunder and news reports that tell only part of the story. We have published the full details to stop the gossip. Olivia and Ben have done nothing they need apologise for.'

Mike Porter was shocked that the profiles had been released but unrepentant about why he had made the assessments in the first place. Drawing a parallel with a very different case, he pointed out that if Auckland police profilers had never looked into the private life of a 'nice cricket umpire' called Peter Plumley Walker they may have never uncovered the strange tale of bondage and dominatrices that lay behind his death.

'Certainly, these ones were not meant to be released, but I have got no problem with them. They were accurate, they were drawn totally from the information. Every bit of the information within those profiles is drawn from someone's statement. I have been accused of picking things out of the air, but that is not right. I drew that information about a young woman that I had no knowledge of from her friends, family and associates. These were all things they'd said.'

The incident, however, did nothing to improve the tense relations between Operation Tam and the families.

However, soon there was a very different problem with a profile. Gerald Hope had obtained a copy of the Watson suspect profile – and he decided to use it to put some pressure on the suspect. He passed it on to a friend of Watson, hoping it would show Watson the police were on his case and encourage him to break. Inevitably it found its way into the hands of Watson's defence team. Gerald Hope also showed the profile to television reporter Kerry Anne Evans, who was making an *Assignment* documentary about the case.

Relations between the police and Hope, often fractured, had reached a low point. Pope frequently had to remind himself, and other members of the team, that Hope's stance was entirely understandable. He was, after all, a grieving parent. Not everything he did was in accord with the investigation's overall aims and sometimes he was highly critical of the police, but Pope was unwilling to be drawn into public disputes with Hope or other members of the family. It would be bad policing – and bad PR. Most of the time when that happened, Pope had to suffer in silence. It would be a while before Pope and Olivia's father sorted out their differences and worked together comfortably again.

Meantime, Operation Tam had more immediate concerns to worry about. In his interview with Fitzgerald, Wallace had also said that the previous Sunday night there had been a band playing at the Punga Cove bar, and one of the crowd there had been Sandy Watson. She had given Wallace a hug and a kiss and told him how the police had their information all wrong and that he, Wallace, was right. Wallace told Fitzgerald that he hadn't had a lot to say to Sandy Watson. 'However, going by his recent behaviour, this is hard to believe,' Fitzgerald said.

Wallace was clearly worth another interview, especially after the media reported him talking about a ketch he had seen in Nelson. This time, on Waitangi Day, it was Detective Sergeant Dave Evans who took Wallace's statement. Wallace told Evans that on a Friday a couple of weeks earlier he had asked to borrow his parents' car. He had told them he was taking it to Blenheim but in fact he had gone to Nelson. He had a friend called Angela, whose partner, Fletch, had just seen moored at Nelson a boat that matched Wallace's description of the one at Furneaux on New Year's Eve. So he decided to check it out. After having a coffee at one of the Nelson cafes, he said, he had headed to the marina on the way out of Nelson toward Motueka, and saw immediately that there were a couple of ketches there. One was called *Waves* and he presumed it was the boat Angela had told him about. It was a very tidy blue and white vessel with a thick wavy line along the side; it didn't look anything like the ketch he had seen at Furneaux. So Wallace said he drove back into Nelson and, from a phone box, rang the Nelson Police Station. Without saying who he was, he told the woman who answered that he was calling about the missing ketch. But she told him the ketch was no longer part of the investigation, and the call ended there.

Now, talking to Evans, Wallace said he regretted he hadn't gone and looked at the other Nelson marina. He had just presumed that the *Waves* was the boat Angela's partner had seen. There were definite similarities, he said, such as the set-up of the rigging and the blue trim around the side, but it wasn't the boat. Still, he was sorry he had not told the woman at the police station about it. He said he wasn't the first person who had experienced a problem being listened to by the Nelson police. He said Don Anderson, from Furneaux, had also drawn a blank when he went to the Nelson station to tell them about the same ketch.

Waves had, in fact, been one of the ketches that Operation Tam had been trying hard to track down, but by now it had been ruled out. Evans showed Wallace a photo of the boat and he correctly identified it; he also identified from a second photo another boat that had been at Furneaux on the night, the *Awesome.*

The police were sceptical about Wallace's latest story. Evans told the briefing that night that he thought Wallace had been telling lies 'from start to finish'. This briefing was attended by Police Commissioner Peter Doone, who was in Blenheim for an update on the inquiry. So this observation about the reliability of the star witness was not offered lightly. 'I'm not sure why he is doing this,' Evans said. And Simon Moore, the detective in charge of the suspect phase of Operation Tam, agreed. 'The more we see of Guy Wallace,' he said, 'the less credible he gets.'

It was agreed that Tom Fitzgerald and Simon Moore would interview Wallace again the next day. This time, at his parents' house in Waikawa Bay, Wallace had a confession to make.

'I would now like to tell the truth,' he said, referring to his visit to Nelson to see the ketch. 'I have not seen this ketch, *Waves*, and I never actually travelled to Nelson on 23 January. I haven't been to Nelson since September 1997.

'I made up the story of seeing *Waves* in Nelson after Don Anderson had told me that he had seen it. I just wanted someone to believe me, and this seemed like a good way of backing my story up. I have been under a lot of pressure from the media, and things got too much for me.'

When Fitzgerald asked Wallace directly if he was still sure about dropping Ben and Olivia off at a ketch, he made his first admission so far that he may have been mistaken. 'I still have this picture in my mind of the ketch,' he said. He had first formed this picture at midday on 2 January when he was asked about the boat by police. 'I can only presume that I formed this image in my mind of the ketch from seeing it when I dropped them off. However, I now know that a number of other people including the Naiad drivers at Furneaux on the night did not see a vessel as I have described. So it is possible I'm mistaken. It surprises me that if a ketch like that was in the inlet that no one else has seen it. I just have this picture in my mind.'

The admission was a breakthrough for police. The key witness was no longer insisting on a boat they couldn't locate. But it had to be taken cautiously, given Wallace's other admission.

And Wallace also had more to say about his encounter with Watson's sister, Sandy. He said he had been sitting in the cabana bar at Punga Cove the previous Sunday having a drink with Julie Roberts – with whom he had apparently made his peace – when he was approached by a young woman who said, 'You're Guy Wallace.'

'Maybe,' he said. 'Who are you?'

When she said she was Sandy Watson, Wallace remembered that he had seen her before at the Toot 'n' Whistle bar, in Picton.

'We have to talk,' Sandy said to Wallace.

They walked down to the jetty and talked for about an hour, on and off. Sandy repeatedly said that the police were wrong and they were trying to frame her brother.

'I said to her that if that was him in the video footage that TVNZ had shown me, and they told me it was Scott Watson, then I would say it wasn't him I dropped off on the yacht.'

Wallace told Fitzgerald that Sandy appeared pretty drunk at the time. 'After our conversation on the jetty, Sandy kissed me. It was a bit more than a friendly kiss – I was a bit taken aback by it. She then got on the Cougar Line boat. It wasn't a passionate kiss, just a bit more than friendly.'

Then Wallace told Fitzgerald that the next day he had received a call from a woman called Beryl, who used to work at the Toot 'n' Whistle. Beryl had told him that Sandy had phoned, telling her to tell Wallace not to try to ring her or see her anywhere, 'because it wouldn't be right'.

The apparent familiarity between Wallace and Sandy Watson was a worry for police. They still hadn't ruled out the possibility of more contact between him and the Watson family. And in the midst of continuing media speculation about past contacts between their key witness and Watson, Wallace added to their worries by remembering a possible meeting with Watson himself.

'Over the past couple of weeks I have been thinking about whether or not I have met any of Beverley Watson's family,' he told Detective Tom Fitzgerald in early March. He said that back in 1994 he had been working as a barman at the Beachcomber

Motor Inn, in Picton. Beverley, Scott Watson's mother, worked in the kitchen at the same time.

'I remember I was working behind the bar. Beverley Watson came into the bar with a male. They weren't drinking in the bar, just walking through. Beverley introduced me to the male as her son. They didn't stay in the bar. She just introduced me and left. I have no recollection of what he looked like or what his name was. I don't know if it was her eldest or youngest son. I am not able to discuss this person as I have no recollection of what he looked like. I have not seen this person since that meeting.

'I first remembered that I had met Beverley's son shortly after I spoke to police on the last occasion a couple of weeks ago, and I have been thinking about it ever since.'

Did that admission amount to a satisfactory limitation of Wallace's acquaintance with Watson to a fleeting, chance encounter, or did it open up a fresh cause for doubt? Police very much hoped it was the former, but they were far from convinced.

Simon Moore wanted to use this meeting with Wallace for another purpose – to test him again on his ketch theory. He took with him a copy of the drawing of the ketch Wallace had drawn for police back in January. Moore placed a pen over the portholes of the ketch and covered the rear mast with his hand and, with the sketch alongside a photo of Watson's boat, asked Wallace if he could see any similarities. Wallace said they looked very similar. But he insisted he had dropped Ben and Olivia at a ketch. It was asking too much to rule out the portholes and rear mast, he said.

Moore told Wallace that police had ruled out the ketch theory because, after all their inquiries, they had found no ketch anchored in the area Wallace had taken the pair to. 'He seemed to come to terms with it but was less than convinced,' Moore noted. He told Wallace to 'put the ketch theory to one side for the time being' and concentrate on the identity of the mystery man who had got off his Naiad with Ben and Olivia. When pressed, he said it was possible the mystery man was Watson, but he didn't know because he couldn't remember what he looked like. But he still remembered the brass portholes on the boat.

Guy Wallace was taking a long time to shape up as a credible witness, but suddenly in early March there appeared to be a breakthrough that might lead to the evidence Operation Tam needed most of all: the bodies of Ben and Olivia.

A fisherman on an expedition just off Tawa Bay, near the eastern head of Endeavour Inlet, pulled up what he thought were strands of thin blonde hair. He and his mates thought it might be important, so they put it on some tissue paper on the deck of their boat to dry, and carried on fishing. But when they returned to Waikawa Bay they were in a hurry to get off the boat, and one of the group, without thinking about it, picked up the paper and the hair and chucked it into a 44-gallon drum along with the rest of their rubbish. About 10 days later they remembered their find and called the police.

By then the contents of the drum were in the Picton rubbish dump. Police decided to search. They established the day on which the contents of the drum had been dumped, and found that that day's rubbish was in an area of about 25 metres by 10 metres. The scene was secured while police worked out how to tackle the dirty job. They asked for about 14 staff from the Woodbourne Air Base to help, and set about two days of sifting through Picton's garbage.

After a day of digging, nothing had been found. However, TV3 reporter Andy Brotherston's crew had meantime over-heard talk of the dump search through a directional microphone while recording another item. TV3's news that night aired the dump search as Operation Tam's possible big breakthrough.

Next day, police decided to bring in a digger to go deeper, and the following day the searchers found most of the material the fishermen had dumped. The samples were dried and sent to the ESR for analysis, and divers were sent down to the point where the men had been fishing. They located a good crop of sea flax – which parts easily and can look like human hair. Operation Tam had struck another dead end.

9

CLOSING IN

$\mathbf{A}$ S THE SUMMER DREW TO A CLOSE with no apparent headway, the media clamour for more information grew louder, along with suggestions that police were on the wrong track altogether. There were also growing signs of impatience from the families. Dick Rolton, who was in charge of relations with the families, frequently had to reassure them that Operation Tam was not being scaled down, and that progress was still being made.

In mid-February Gerald Hope rang the Operation Tam headquarters to say he had received a call from TV3 reporter Andy Brotherston. She had asked if he knew that the forensic examination of the *Blade* had produced no results because the boat had been so thoroughly wiped down. The information, she said, had come from a 'Tony' who was in charge of the Wellington end of Operation Tam. In Blenheim, police knew of no such Tony. The call was a worrying breach of security and, worse, added to the difficulties of dealing with the families.

While the searching was being scaled down, there was still plenty going on behind the scenes – some of it very much behind the scenes. An amendment to the Crimes Act came into effect on 1 February, removing the requirement for police to suspect a conspiracy of at least six people before they could install bugging devices to gather evidence. The law now allowed Operation Tam more leeway to bug some likely sources of information. Watson's boat, which had been returned to him, was wired, as were a number of houses and telephones, around both Picton and the North Island, where Watson had travelled as the inquiry was heating up behind him.

Around the same time, police found that the *Blade* had disappeared from Shakespeare Bay. It appeared that Watson was on the run from Operation Tam. Through a process of elimination they had a Christchurch team watch Lyttelton Harbour and they saw the boat pull in one Sunday afternoon. It had been repainted, and now was white. From the team's reports, police were pretty sure that Watson's father and brother, Chris and Tom, were on board. Watson himself had earlier been in Christchurch and had been seen on a Christchurch City Council's security camera at a McDonald's outlet in Colombo Street. Police were trying to obtain a copy of the security video to identify Watson. If they could get a good still shot from the video footage, it may be useful in seeking witnesses' identification of Watson.

By late June police decided they had got everything they were going to get from the wires and they were unhooked. From the hours of tape, there were only a few comments that might be useful. Watson, police presumed, had been told by his lawyer that his conversations could be tapped, and was being careful. Watson's lawyer, Bruce Davidson, had in fact given him precisely that advice.

'We gave him the usual kind of warnings. We said you have to be aware that the police have the ability to obtain warrants to search properties and bug houses and bug telephones. And we told him he should not only be concerned about approaches by the police, but that, for example, his girlfriend could well be someone who he should not talk to. Because even something said to her quite innocently could be misconstrued and used against him. That's all pretty standard advice really.'

Davidson, of Wellington, had been on Watson's case since January. A Blenheim firm of solicitors had originally been acting for Watson but when it became clear that Watson was a prime suspect they decided that he needed someone from outside the district.

'They obviously made a decision fairly promptly that whoever looked after his interests during the course of the investigation should be someone from outside the Blenheim area – because of the small size of the community,' Davidson said. 'There were obvious difficulties, one would have thought, for any local lawyer in becoming too involved – there was huge public sympathy for the families involved.' The Blenheim lawyers had a more specific potential conflict of interest. The firm acted for the Marlborough District Council, where Gerald Hope was a councillor, and they saw a very difficult situation ahead if they were ever to go to trial.

They approached Davidson and fellow Wellington lawyer John Billington, QC, who had represented John Barlow through his three trials before he was convicted of the double murder of Wellington businessmen Eugene and Gene Thomas. But as the case progressed Billington, in Davidson's words, 'more or less faded out of it. I imagine he was left gutted after the Barlow case, and wondered whether physically he had the energy to get up and do such a thing again.'

By the time Davidson was taken on, Watson had already made a couple of long statements to the police, so the options for any defence case were already limited. By then, too, media interest in every aspect of the case was intense. But Davidson was determined to be matter-of-fact about it. He took on fellow Wellington defence lawyer Mike Antunovic to work on the case with him. Antunovic was a keen boatie with good knowledge of the Marlborough Sounds, and he was used to cases that attracted a lot of media hype.

'Mike and I have tried continually to remind ourselves that this is just another case. We approach it in the same way as we've approached any case. The danger is that if you get into a spin about it, you might take shortcuts, you might get involved in the media hype. Sure, there's a hell of a lot of interest in it and sure, there's a hell of a lot of evidence, but you treat it in the same way that you treat any other case.'

But obviously it wasn't any other case in terms of the mountain of evidence that was being built up because of the very large number of witnesses being interviewed. Early on, Davidson decided to hire private investigators to try to get a fix on the sort of information the police may be compiling. Later on, the private investigators would be able to help sift through the information that would come to the defence as part of the prosecution's disclosure of evidence. Davidson went to a Wellington firm, Corporate Risks, which was run by a former policeman, Quentin Doig. At the start the private investigators' costs were met by the Watson family.

'Over January and February the PIs conducted a relatively limited investigation of their own, which involved talking to various witnesses or potential witnesses in the Blenheim and the Marlborough Sounds area.' Davidson wanted the investigators to talk to the potential witnesses as soon as possible while they still could. Once any charges were laid, there would be legal and ethical constraints on the people they could talk to.

'One thing became clear very quickly. The private investigation revealed the difficulties the police were having with the nub of the eye-witness evidence. There was certainly conflicting evidence about the identity of the person the kids got onto the boat with. The investigation didn't reveal any secrets, but it made it pretty obvious early on in the piece the kind of difficulties the police must have been encountering for themselves.

'It meant for me representing him that by the time the investigators had completed their report we had a reasonable insight into some of the areas that would be important, in particular the events at Furneaux Lodge itself.'

Police were uneasy about the arrival of private investigators on the scene, more so because the media seemed to know about their presence as soon as the police did. But Quentin Doig seemed to want to be up-front about his activities. In February he phoned Operation Tam's second in command, John Rae, to say that he had been hired by the solicitor acting for Watson's family and that he and an off-sider, Carl Berryman, another former policeman, would be arriving in Blenheim in a couple of days. They wanted to meet Pope and Rae to assure them that they would be acting responsibly and that 'there would be no underhand dealing'.

They agreed to meet at a local restaurant, Bellafico's. At the meeting, Pope expressed his concern that the PIs' activities had been made public. Doig was at pains to say he had been hounded by the media, and reiterated his message that they would be acting responsibly. Pope asked that the meeting, and any subsequent conversations, be kept confidential. Doig and Berryman agreed to that and said they had been given a list of people to interview, and would be trying to obtain copies of their statements to police. Doig appeared to offer to co-operate with the police, saying he was unsure how to deal with any information he came across that might be helpful to the police. He said he was under instructions to pass on any information first to the defence solicitors, but seemed to leave open the possibility of giving it to police.

Pope may have been reassured by the meeting, but he still wanted his team to keep an eye on what the private investigators were doing. The next day he told the team that all movements of the two men should be logged, and asked that they make sure any witnesses they spoke to were aware of the implications of talking to them.

Operation Tam took the registration number of the car the two were travelling in and began to compile a log of 'Sightings of Doig & Berryman'. The log showed that the PIs' inquiries were pretty similar to those of the police themselves. Doig visited a neighbour of Watson, for example, and asked what he could see in Watson's backyard. They talked about how the Watson family believed Scott was innocent, but that he was the black sheep of the family, with a bit of a chequered past. It appeared, too, that many of the people the PIs spoke to were happy to pass on their conversations to Operation Tam. A witness from Endeavour Inlet rang the police as soon as Doig and Berryman called her to say they wanted to pay a visit. She told police she didn't intend to talk to them and would ask them to leave. Another witness, who had helped with the Hope and Smart families' boat searches, gave the PIs the same message when they showed him the suspect profile police had prepared on Scott Watson. He told police that Berryman indicated he was heading back to Wellington soon.

In fact, much of the Corporate Risks' work for Davidson was undertaken in Wellington. After they had completed fairly basic investigations in Marlborough they headed back to get down to the long, hard slog of sifting through all the information that the prosecution team eventually began passing on to the defence. By law, police and the eventual prosecution team are required to pass on to the defence all material information they gather, whether it is used as evidence or not. The defence team sifts through the information, trying to find evidence the police may have overlooked or downplayed, or looking for possible doubts to sow in the minds of the jury. Since Watson's arrest, the prosecution had been passing on information. The document flow would later become a torrent as the case went to depositions.

To Davidson, such assistance was vital. 'It was an absolute necessity. If the case was simply a routine one where defendant X was charged with rape, for example, you'd do this work yourself. There would be a few files coming in and you might be looking at a two- or three-day trial with, say, 20 witnesses. You'd be faced with a foolscap folder of disclosure material. Any lawyer regularly doing defence work could organise that himself in a few hours. Here it was so vastly different simply because of the sheer size. It would have been impossible for me or any other solicitor to organise the disclosure, short of taking three or four months off work.'

Once disclosure proper was under way, the prosecution was passing on its thousands of files on disks. There was so much to sort through, pulling out basic information and arranging it in useful order, that Corporate Risks hired students from Student Job Search to do a lot of the leg work. Their rate, $12 an hour, was a whole lot cheaper than any lawyer's.

As the long hot summer of 1998 turned to a long dry autumn, police were still publicly insisting there was no prime suspect in Operation Tam. But while they were still working hard on eliminating people from the long list of possible suspects, members of the team co-ordinated by analyst Mike Porter and Detective Senior Sergeant Wayne Stringer were trying to leave no stone unturned in their attempt to build a full picture of Scott Watson. Police in other parts of the country were asked to contact Watson's former cellmates from his spells in prison to see what he had talked about, how he had behaved, and whether he had any traits that could have motivated him to kill Ben and Olivia. There were also intermittent inquiries within the Marlborough drug scene to establish whether Watson had any links there. But although some people who spoke to police said he had a 'huge' drug habit, Watson didn't seem to fit into that community. Stringer spent a lot of time talking to junkies and chemists but he reported that Watson was 'not known at all in that fraternity'.

Nevertheless, by late March the Operation Tam team had prepared a comprehensive 'preliminary profile' on Watson.

Whether this psychological assessment could implicate Watson in the deaths of Ben and Olivia was a question that would yet have to be argued, but it certainly painted a grim picture of a man who was anti-social, obsessive, a binge drinker and drug taker and often a pretty nasty piece of work. He had served a 14-month prison sentence in 1990. Most of his time was served in Invercargill Prison, but before his release he was transferred to Rolleston, near Christchurch.

Police had heard that while in Invercargill Prison Watson had attacked a pastor with a knife. Unfortunately, the pastor had subsequently died, and the attack was not reported as a criminal offence, so there was nothing on file. Pope also learned that he had impaled a fellow inmate with a piece of four-by-two with a nail on the end, but again there was nothing police could use. Pope believed the incidents certainly showed Watson to be a 'vicious little toad, a fiery, peppery bloke'.

It added up to a picture of an objectionable character, although it wasn't in itself extraordinary. But police also found some people with stories to tell about Watson that pointed to a genuinely menacing streak. And their stories weren't about prison incidents nearly a decade earlier, but behaviour in the Marlborough Sounds, just a few days before New Year's Day, 1998.

One of the people was a young Christchurch Telecom worker, Simon Skelton, who had been camping at Momorangi Bay, in the headwaters of Queen Charlotte Sound, between Christmas and New Year with his wife Jenny and their friends Debbie and Gary Cassidy. One afternoon Simon and Gary had returned after water-skiing to find that Debbie had two guests at their site in the camp. She introduced them to Simon as Scott and Sandy. Debbie Cassidy had remembered Sandy from years ago, when both were in the fourth form at Hornby High School, on the outskirts of Christchurch. The Watsons were then living on a boat moored in Lyttelton Harbour. Once, during the fifth form year, Sandy had announced that the family was sailing to Chile. They disappeared, but a few days later Sandy turned up at school again – her mother had become seasick and the trip was cancelled.

Sandy Watson and Debbie Cassidy had kept loosely in touch since their school days. Over the years, Debbie had got to know Scott as well. She met him at Sandy's 21st, at Rolleston, and soon learned that he was constantly in some sort of trouble, often with the law. Debbie had also attended Sandy's wedding in 1989, to a guy from the army. Then, in about mid-1997, Debbie received a card from Sandy saying she and the two little girls she had had moved to Marlborough. The card had only Sandy's name on it, so Debbie presumed Sandy's husband was no longer on the scene. She sent Sandy a card, telling her she was going to be in Momorangi Bay over Christmas. She thought they might go and see Sandy and the girls one day, but didn't expect to see them at the campsite.

The group spent the rest of the afternoon and the evening sitting around drinking beer, but Sandy and Scott wanted some harder stuff and went back to the boat at one stage and returned with a 750ml bottle of Coruba rum and some Coke. The two of them rapidly drank all the rum and most of the Coke, while Scott talked about how he had built his boat and travelled around the North Island. He invited the group out for a sail the following day. There was talk of Scott maybe sailing to Tonga one day. Simon Skelton didn't think that Scott's 'ugly' little yacht – which he later recognised on TV, though by then it was blue rather then reddish – would make it to Tonga. He couldn't work out whether Sandy was intending to go as well or whether Scott was trying to talk her into it.

Scott talked about a friend of his whom Skelton took to be a dope grower, and they talked about incidents such as the time Scott and Sandy were 'drunk as skunks' and had let off a flare which started a fire in the bush. As the night and the alcohol wore on, Gary noticed the way Scott and Sandy reacted to each other. 'I thought they were very close, bordering on strange – as if they were lovers or something,' Skelton told police. 'We all talked or passed a comment about the way they acted with each other the day after, and thought it was really strange to say the least.

'As the evening developed and Scott consumed the rum, his personality changed. He became loud, obnoxious, boasting about getting away with a lot without paying for it.'

By this time Watson had started having Debbie Cassidy on about her hair: she used to have shoulder-length blonde hair but had changed it to a red bob and Watson didn't like it. He kept on repeating that she shouldn't have changed her hair because it was better long and blonde. 'I got the impression Scott liked Debbie, and particularly blonde hair,' Skelton said. He put the behaviour down to too much alcohol in short order, but he knew Debbie wasn't happy with the comments. Watson also mocked Debbie's glasses, calling her 'four-eyes'.

'By this time I was getting uncomfortable being with Scott. He was getting drunker and drunker and I was getting scared of him. I wanted him away and out of the campsite,' Skelton said. 'I was scared because he looked confrontational. He was lean, had a couple of days' stubble, olive skinned, tattoos on his forearms, and I was a bit wary of him. When we first met him he seemed okay but when he was drunk his whole personality changed and I didn't like him.'

Debbie Cassidy was certainly getting sick of Watson as the evening wore on. She remembered him being so drunk he kept asking her to roll his cigarettes for him, and he seemed obsessed with her blonde hair and with the leopardskin top she had worn at Sandy's 21st all those years ago.

'He moved his chair closer to me and shut himself off from the rest of the conversation and the rest of the group. He began focusing all his attention on me. He wasn't being abusive but he swore a lot. His behaviour was just annoying. I didn't fear for my own safety because Gary was there and he was drunk – Scott I mean,' she recalled. Mainly, Debbie was embarrassed for Sandy, because Sandy was her friend and her brother was behaving so badly. Eventually, Debbie got so sick of Watson she asked him to leave.

Shortly after he was given the shove, Watson 'appeared out of nowhere' beside another tent in the campsite where another woman, whose name cannot be used, was staying with a family group. He was clutching a badly rolled cigarette and asking for a light. The woman's brother-in-law gave him a light and she offered him a seat because he was lurching about so much that she was worried he was going to set the place on fire with his smoke. Then a woman appeared. 'What the hell are you up to?' she asked the guy. She had obviously been drinking too, but she made more sense than he did and the camper soon found out that the pair were brother and sister, called Scott and Sandy. It was an odd scene outside the tent – the woman camper wrapped in a blanket, and the rest of the group listening to a scarcely coherent couple who had stumbled onto the scene.

'She did most of the talking and the guy Scott sat in his chair with his head sort of bowed, like he was pretty drunk. Every now and then he would put his head up and have a bit of a yak.'

Watson was reasonably coherent about his boat, however. He said it had cost him $12,000 to build in his backyard, and he was particularly proud of the navigation gear he had on board. He offered to take them out on the boat the next morning. He also brought up the idea of a trip to Tonga, saying he would go when the trade winds were right, probably in about June.

The woman and her group had been talking with Watson for only about half an hour when he made what she thought was an odd suggestion: 'Hey, you in the blanket, I want you to come on board and cook my breakfast. You be my cook.' Then he pointed to her brother-in-law and said, 'You be my crew.'

The woman decided it was the drink talking. 'He was pretty drunk and he kept repeating what he said, like he would ask me, "What do you think about that, what do you think about that, you the one in the blanket?"'

Watson said he had changed the name of his boat – the woman thought it had been *Chandlair* or something like that – because when he had mentioned the name to some guys in a Napier bar they had told him it was the name of a faggot movie. Watson said he had removed the old name and now called the boat *Mad Dog*. He kept yelling 'Mad Dog', again and again during the conversation. Then he started ranting: 'Got to kill the dog, kill the dog.' He was highly agitated, punching his fist in the air as he said it.

The brother-in-law noticed Watson had two fingers missing and asked how it happened. But Watson went surly and said, 'Oh, you noticed them, did you?' before changing the subject. Eventually, this group too got tired of Watson and his 'creepy' overtures, and they stood up and said it was time to go to bed. Watson and his sister stumbled off into the night, heading towards the bay.

But that wasn't quite the end of the evening. They had hardly left when Sandy fell over, so a couple of the campers helped her to her feet. As they turned to go back to their tent, Watson noticed them and yelled, 'No. You're coming on my boat. You're coming on my boat.' But the brother-in-law told them to ignore him, and just keep walking back to the tent. Once inside, they stayed awake for a long time in case the Watsons returned. Fortunately, they didn't.

Later, the scene would seem like an eerie preview of New Year's night when Watson, drunk and obnoxious, was keen to get another young woman on board his boat. The next morning, when they looked out to the bay, Watson and his boat had disappeared.

Another person was located with a sobering story about Watson. She was a young woman from Picton whose husband had worked with Watson occasionally at Carey's Boat Yard. Watson had sometimes helped the couple with work on their boat, and one day in November 1997 he turned up unexpectedly at their house. Watson and the guy sat down for a few drinks while the man's wife went out. When she got back late in the afternoon, they were both out on the balcony still drinking and both 'pretty merry'. They were talking about a trip on Watson's boat, and Watson said one of the guys on board had had a lot of 'kinky toys' and some dirty movies. The woman heard talk of animals and movies where people got killed. She presumed they were talking about snuff movies. 'I don't need to hear about this,' the woman thought.

'Scott talked about it for probably half an hour, I suppose. I remember Scott saying that the guy with all this stuff was meant to be really rich. The gist of what I picked up from Scott was that there were a lot of weird things going on on the boat. It was definitely more than just a group of guys watching a few blue movies. I said I didn't want to hear any more and stood up and walked away.' So Watson and her husband decided to go down to the pub, much to the woman's relief.

'I was quite happy to see them go . . . and happy to get rid of Scott. They weren't really drunk, just loud and well on their way to being pissed. They had probably had about a dozen cans and a bottle of wine. I think they went to the Federal. They were gone for about two hours.'

While they were away, the woman noticed a knife Watson had left behind, a flick-knife with a four-inch silver blade. She fiddled with it for a while.

'When they arrived back they were very merry. They weren't that drunk that they were falling over or anything and I could understand their speech quite clearly,' she said. They were talking about what had happened at the Federal, where the only other person in the bar had been a lone woman.

After they had been there for a while the female started pestering them. The man said that he thought she was a prostitute. 'They apparently started being rude to her, saying things like, "Show us your tits," and carrying on. Scott was going on about how she was a real dog. At about that stage Scott started saying something to the effect of how they should have bumped her off.

'I can't remember how it came up but Scott started going on about murder and how easy it would be. He started going on about if I wanted anyone murdered he would do it for me. He had this real evil look in his eye and he was very intense. It takes a bit to make me nervous, but the way he was talking was making me scared. He seemed to have psyched himself into it.

'Every time I changed the subject he would bring it back to murder. I got the impression that if I had said to him, "Go and murder the girl in the pub," he would have done it.'

The next morning the couple talked about what had happened and the husband agreed that Watson had been a bit freaky. And he certainly hadn't liked the way Watson had spoken to his wife about killing someone. The woman told him that she didn't want Watson back at their house again. They also noticed that Watson had left his knife behind. After the way Watson had talked, they didn't want it in their home. Nor did they want him coming back to get it, so the man made a point of taking the knife straight to Watson's sister's house, where he left it on the veranda.

The woman thought of that night a couple of months later when she heard about the two kids who had gone missing at Furneaux Lodge.

'As soon as I read it I thought of Scott. I know my husband thought of Scott too when he read it.'

As he worked on the Watson profile, Wayne Stringer believed the picture that was emerging was certainly convincing enough to put Watson right at the middle of the disappearance of Ben and Olivia. He drew up a summary list of the characteristics Watson displayed and it wasn't a pretty list:

- Solitary character
- No formal period of socialisation with peers as a child
- No strong bonds or allegiance to family other than to Sandy
- History of alcohol and drug abuse
- History of impulsive, opportunistic offending
- Compulsive thief
- No work ethic
- Arrogant
- Sarcastic
- Anti-authority
- Internal rationalisation of actions; projection of blame on society or others
- Obsessive victimisation of weaker individuals
- Distrust/dislike of women
- No apparent stable relationships with women
- Periods of impotence
- Self-gratification as his prime motivation
- No social conscience
- Ingrained racial, ethnic, religious prejudices and active discrimination
- Irrational impulsive violent acts
- Fascination with knives.

Mike Porter, the analyst, had also done his own work assessing Watson's characteristics. He had pulled together his assessment of Watson's mood swings during the events of the New Year's party, and linked them with the stimulants he was drinking and smoking to build up a possible narrative of what Watson had done, and why.

As Porter told it, Watson set off from Picton and sailed to Endeavour Inlet in a buoyant and expectant mood, fuelled by a mounting intake of booze and dope. On shore at Furneaux, he was told to get rid of his bottle, so he skulled the lot, feeling angry and embarrassed at being caught out. Porter believed that throughout the early part of the evening Watson developed a staunch and angry attitude as he sat in the bar drinking, unable to relate to or break into any of the established groups there. He grew alternatively argumentative and withdrawn as the evening progressed, picking the odd fight, and coming on abrasive and macho. Unable to pick up any company for the night, particularly female company, he took to drinking more double bourbons and rum and Cokes, withdrawing into himself and out of synch with the party atmosphere.

Porter depicted Watson as totally drunk by the time he made his way back to the *Blade*, but still wanting to party. He conjectured that Watson's mood lifted when he found himself on the water taxi with the young Ben and Olivia, and that he made a genuine offer of a bed when he heard of their plight. He believed Watson would have been buoyant when he got them on board, possibly sharing a drink and a smoke with them.

But his mood would have turned to dejection when Olivia and Ben decided they wanted to turn in for the night. Still wanting to party, and wanting some female company, Watson made visits to a couple of vessels moored alongside. But again he was rejected. Everyone was settling down for the night and he still hadn't scored.

Porter depicted Watson as raging with anger and hate when he returned to the *Blade*. Feeling alone and rejected, he decided to untie his vessel and leave the inlet. Ben and Olivia were probably asleep, unaware that the *Blade* was leaving Furneaux, Porter suggested.

Porter believed that it was only then that Watson, still fuming about his rejection, realised he had a captive audience down below and started to get ideas about Olivia. Possibly he argued with Olivia when she woke up – she was known to be argumentative. Porter believed Watson would have reacted violently to her attitude and the scene may have wakened the sleeping Ben.

What would have happened then? The notes in Porter's assessment suggest a horrible narrative for the one part of the story that had never, could never be told by anyone except Watson, if police's suspicions were right: 'Ben also awake. Possibly dealt to with knife. Overpowers Ben and Olivia and contains both. Rapes Olivia. Olivia's torment may be over an extended period.'

When the full horror of his actions hit him, Watson would have been seized with a mix of panic and the need to plan, to cover his tracks, Porter suggested. So he looked for refuge in familiar territory, heading to Erie Bay and Te Weuweu Bay, where he'd been many times. He had to dump or conceal the bodies and the evidence. Porter believed he had a couple of choices. Tory Channel was very deep. And he knew the bush area very well from his cannabis growing.

After thoroughly cleaning and repainting the *Blade*, and believing he had successfully covered his tracks, Watson would have assumed a mounting belief in himself, convincing himself that he was untouchable, that his crime would never be discovered, Porter suggested. Back in Picton, especially once he saw Sandy again, his sense of self-denial grew as he started putting about stories to match his own sequence of events.

There was no way of knowing whether this was a plausible narrative, a credible recreation of Watson's state of mind. Many of the elements of the story would remain forever in the realm of conjecture. Those elements could never be put directly to a jury, but only be left to them to infer from the gaps in the story police might be able to tell. But were there still too many holes in the story to make a credible prosecution?

As police tried to flesh out Watson's story, there were some other tantalising leads. One concerned American woman Nancy Frey, heir to Hershey's chocolate empire, who went missing from Great Barrier Island in September 1997. From as early as February, Operation Tam had been aware that Watson had been up near Great Barrier at the time, on his trip around the North Island. The team investigating Frey's death believed she had either been killed or accidentally fallen and drowned. If it was homicide, then Watson's movements in the area were worth investigation, Pope and his team believed. A search of Watson's bank records established that he had made transactions in Whangarei on 21 September and 24 September. He was as close as a comfortable day's sailing away from the place where Frey had disappeared. A copy of the psychological assessment of Watson and his bank records were sent to the Frey inquiry team.

The suggestions about Watson's possible involvement were 'purely a matter of timing', Pope said. Although just incidental, they were not dismissed until they had been properly checked. 'We spoke to the officer in charge of that case, and he was quite interested in his movements. We fed the information we had through the Auckland group and they carried out their inquiries. He was in the area all right, and he was seen in the company of a female, but in the end it didn't pan out.

'That's not unusual in inquiries like this. You often spread out and link up with other inquiries. You need to keep your mind open to those possibilities, especially when you're dealing with someone of the ilk of Watson. He's not like a bloke who'd be a stranger to that type of offending.'

But in the end Watson had a definite alibi: he was off the scene, at Parua Bay, near Whangarei, at the relevant time.

By late March police felt their case against Watson was beginning to harden up. They were also coming to the realisation that the strong presence of Operation Tam in Marlborough might be coming to the end of its useful life. So they decided to quit the Operation Tam headquarters in Seymour Street from 31 March. They would move out over the last weekend of the month and thoroughly clean out the office overnight on Monday 30 March, leaving the place just as they had found it. A downsized Operation Tam headquarters was set up in the Telecom building next to the Blenheim Police Station. It was to stay in the new headquarters until late May, when Tam moved back to Christchurch.

As they moved out of Seymour Street, Pope reviewed the inquiry to date. He wrote to his police bosses with a summary of Operation Tam so far; and the facts he pulled together showed something of the size of the operation – and the questions that still had to be answered.

In all, 130 people had been nominated as suspects. Of them, 129 had been definitely eliminated because they had little known association with the events as they had been established. One principal suspect remained – Scott Watson.

Along with Pope and his second in command, John Rae and Detective Dick Rolton in Blenheim, who would stay in charge of managing the Tam file, four detectives based in Christchurch would remain dedicated to Operation Tam. Another Christchurch detective would remain in charge of any searching that still needed to be done and a team of six detectives from Christchurch and Dunedin would continue the work of interviewing witnesses. In all, 1634 witnesses had been identified, and 299 were yet to be interviewed, mainly in Christchurch and Wellington. They aimed to complete their inquiries by the end of April.

The yacht phase of the inquiry was left in the hands of Detective Bruce McLachlan, who had been working with Wayne Stringer on the yachts since the beginning. Stringer believed he had identified all the owners of the boats at Furneaux over New Year and had finished about 80 percent of his inquiries with them. Two other staff would stay on the case, looking after general logistics and the co-ordination of exhibits.

But the police were also picking up suggestions that they might not get much more against Watson until he was arrested. Locals, they learned, were fearful of coming forward with information until he was actually named as a suspect and charges were laid. Only then, police were told, might people be prepared to come forward with incriminating material.

Police faced a conundrum. Should they arrest Watson with the material they had so far and hope it held up in court, or should they hold out for a stronger case? While they waited, there was always the risk that Watson would do a runner or use the time with his lawyers to build up a sturdier defence case. When should they jump?

10

THE ARREST

THE SUMMER OF BEN'S AND OLIVIA'S disappearance was long gone, and Rob Pope and the Operation Tam team faced a grim winter. But the cold weather at last brought some momentum to the investigation. By May, the police's legal experts believed they were amassing a strong case against Scott Watson. And out on the waters of the Marlborough Sounds there were signs that all the searching was about to hit pay-dirt.

For months, police divers had been searching the Sounds, concentrating on areas where the *Blade* had been seen on New Year's Day or soon after. The Wellington police launch, *Lady Elizabeth 3*, had come over for several forays, and from the start much of their interest had centred on Marine Head, where Endeavour Inlet opens into Queen Charlotte Sound. Police had witnesses who had seen the *Blade* near Marine Head early in the morning of New Year's Day and then a little later at Kurakura Point, further up Queen Charlotte Sound.

'Those sightings of the *Blade* gave us confidence that if the bodies were not far out at sea, then Endeavour Inlet or its mouth was the area where it's most likely they or the kids' clothing had been dumped,' Pope said. 'We had two or three sightings of the *Blade* either anchored or moving very slowly. The area obviously warranted a close examination.' One sighting, in particular, was of a boat that looked like the *Blade* stalled in the area and of a man looking over the edge down into the water. Had he just dumped something over the side?

By late March the police divers had found nothing, and a decision was made to bring in more sophisticated searching equipment. Pope began locating operators of sonar equipment and remotely operated underwater vehicles that could carry out a video search of the sea bed. In May, Pope got the green light to contract the Navy's HMNZS *Wakakura* which was equipped with sonar and a submersible, remotely operated rig. Some parts of the Sounds are up to 70 metres deep, and the *Wakakura*'s diving equipment meant the divers could go far deeper than the police divers could. With a recompression chamber, they could go down to at least 50 metres.

Initially, they would search the mouth of Endeavour Inlet, from Marine Head to Scott Point and across to Blumine Island. If the sonar scanning found objects of interest, it could then be checked by divers or the remote.

But the search was never going to be easy. Otago University sonar expert Chris Spiers had helped survey the same area several years before and knew what the Navy should expect. 'We found very heavy sediment on the bottom at Endeavour Inlet. It's a muddy, gooey consistency. Objects tend to settle into it. In the [Queen Charlotte] Sound itself there's a lot of tidal movement that keeps it scoured out more. Side-scan sonar gives you a photocopy type image of what's down there – the challenge is trying to interpret what you see,' Spiers said. If there were bodies tied to some sort of weight, the human remains were not likely to be identifiable as such, but the weight might be picked up by sonar, showing where to head for a closer search.

From the start the Navy searchers found plenty of objects down on the muddy sea bed, including a submerged dinghy, but none of them seemed to have any significance. From about 40 findings, about 10 were identified as warranting a further examination, although Pope still wasn't attaching any particular significance to them.

But then in mid-May the video scanning detected an apparently sensational find – an object on the seabed that looked a lot like two bodies wrapped in some sort of shroud.

Pope was stunned by the video images. So was a police pathologist who was brought up from Dunedin to look at the images. He agreed it looked like two wrapped bodies. If these were the bodies of Ben and Olivia, it would be the breakthrough that Operation Tam had been looking for since January. Complex logistics were put in place to bring the object to the surface.

'It involved a huge amount or preparatory work,' Pope said. 'We had to prepare on the basis that this was bodies. While the water may have preserved them to a degree, as soon as they were exposed to oxygen there was the advice that they would rapidly decompose. We had a three-tonne truck packed with ice in a discrete little bay a couple of ks away.'

The object would be winched to the surface in a wire cradle, lifted by a crane on board the Wellington dive support vessel *Seawatch*. A boat was standing by to take it immediately to the ice-packed truck which would ferry it immediately to Wellington for examination by the pathologists.

Ben's and Olivia's families were warned about the discovery. Police realised this would be a hard time for them, however it turned out. Whether at last they were to find their children's bodies or have their hopes dashed yet again, they were going to need a lot of support. Police rang Father Barry Scannell, Mary Smart's former parish priest, who had shifted to Auckland. They wanted to make sure he at least would be in touch with John and Mary when the news, whatever it might be, came through.

On Saturday 16 May all the plans were in place to lift the object. Police had been tight-lipped about their activities and a security cordon was put in place around the operation. But inevitably word had got out that Operation Tam was about to have a sensational breakthrough. And just as inevitably, the cameras got close enough to record the large object as it was lifted on board the *Seawatch*, in the early afternoon sun, dripping water and sediment.

The observers who had gathered around in small boats – and there were plenty of them – were convinced that police had at last discovered the bodies. 'I think they've found what they were looking for,' a water taxi driver told reporters. 'I never thought they'd find something like that. I was expecting small items, perhaps jewellery or personal effects. Nothing as big as that.'

But when the crane got the catch on board and police got close enough to have a good look, all the hopes were deflated. It was a sail, with nothing inside. The body-like shapes were just a fluke of how the sail had come to rest on the sea bed.

Ben's and Olivia's families watched the news of the recovery on the television news that evening, still waiting to hear the worst from the police. Pope was still not giving anything away publicly. 'We don't know how relevant it is until we have examined it. Until you can isolate it from where it is and carefully examine it, you don't know,' he said. 'It'll be some time before we do know that.'

Privately, he was devastated. 'I was absolutely gutted, I think more for the families' sake than anything else. Because it really struck home how much emotional turmoil they were in, but trying to suppress it. We had finally given them an indication that there may be some hope of finding something, and then we let them down. It was a sad day.'

The sail turned out to have an owner – Outward Bound. 'The most expensive sail recovery in the Sounds,' Pope noted.

Despite the setback, Rob Pope believed Operation Tam was ready to 'turn the key' and arrest Scott Watson. The investigation, he thought, had yielded as much as it was ever going to. He believed Operation Tam had conclusively proved that Ben and Olivia had been murdered. It was also extremely unlikely that the bodies or any other associated evidence would ever be found, so the case for arresting Watson was as good as it was going to get. Now it was time to act.

Virtually everybody who had been at Furneaux Lodge and Endeavour Inlet that night had been found and interviewed. About 130 suspects had been investigated, but Scott Watson stood out beyond them all. Through the things he had done, the lies and inconsistent explanations he had given for his behaviour, and the location of the *Blade* on the night – and its movements and clean-up afterwards – Watson had emerged as the only person who could not be discounted as the man responsible for the murders.

When he reviewed them, Pope believed that Watson's statements to police were littered with lies and inconsistencies.

'I was clean-shaven. I had a shave that day,' Watson had said. But 16 witnesses identified him as unshaven on New Year's Eve, and a video taken at Furneaux showed he had stubble.

'I was wearing blue jeans, and white and black Bianchi shoes. I was wearing a grey jersey with two red stripes across the chest. I also had on a grey tee-shirt that had "Ocean Spirit" written on it,' Watson claimed. But nine witnesses said he had been wearing a denim shirt, and he had been photographed wearing it.

'At about 2 a.m. I took the water taxi back to my yacht. I was the only passenger,' Watson said. But numerous witnesses identified him at Furneaux until 4 a.m. and no water taxi driver took a lone passenger out to the boats until after then.

'I left Furneaux at about 7 a.m.,' Watson said. But four witnesses said he left the inlet between 5.30 a.m. and 6.30 a.m.

'I sailed to Erie Bay in the Tory Channel. I visited my boss's house . . . I suppose I got to Erie Bay about half past nine or 10 o'clock on New Year's Day.' But the *Blade* did not arrive at Erie Bay until after 5 p.m.

Watson's former girlfriend had also strengthened the case against Watson, police believed. 'I have asked Scott if he had anything to do with those two people going missing and he has said that he had nothing to do with it,' she had told police. 'He did offer a suggestion as to where they might be now though. He said, "They will be in Cook Strait."'

And: 'I asked Scott if he was trying to pick up women on New Year's Eve and he admitted that he was, although he has never said anything else at all about what he did on New Year's Eve . . . '

And: 'We never really talked about the case at all but right out of the blue he asked me if I knew about the hatch. I had not mentioned anything about it at all . . . I asked him what he meant and he said that there were scratch-marks on the rubber inside the hatch that had been caused by his sister's children, Hannah and Lisa, and he thought that is why the police took it away.'

Then there was Watson's comment to his former girlfriend, after the *Assignment* programme, when he had said Olivia hated her father and couldn't wait to get away from him. 'I was horrified by this as it sounded to me like he had been talking to Olivia,' the girlfriend told police. 'My feelings must have shown in my face as Scott then quickly said, "That's what her friends were saying anyway."'

But if he was to take the case to trial, Pope would have to deal with the tricky question of the ketch Guy Wallace claimed to have delivered Ben and Olivia to. The police would have to build up a case proving that Wallace was wrong about the ketch but right about what else he remembered from the night. The police would have to show that Watson was the stranger who boarded Guy Wallace's Naiad water taxi at about 4 a.m., and that he got off with Ben and Olivia onto his boat – and both these propositions were a little problematic given Wallace's evidence. Wallace had described the person who got onto the Naiad as the same person who he had served double bourbons in the bar throughout the evening. The stranger had told Wallace he was from Picton. But when Wallace had been shown a photographic montage, he had not selected Watson. He had, however, picked out Watson when later shown another photographic montage. As for the boat, there was no dispute that the Naiad water taxi had taken Rick Goddard and Amelia Hope and the man from Furneaux Jetty to the *Tamarack* and ultimately Ben and Olivia to a boat where the three got off. And from piecing together the positions of all the boats in Endeavour Inlet, there was no doubt about where precisely the *Blade* had been on New Year's night. Hope, Smart and Watson alighted. Photos from witnesses had positively identified the *Blade* in the inlet, rafted up to the *Mina Cornelia* and *Bianco*, in the vicinity where Wallace had delivered the three. More photos had shown the *Blade* was definitely gone by 6 a.m. But of course there would be the old ketch question to address.

No ketch had been seen by anyone in the position where Wallace took the three people on the water taxi. Five other ketches had been moored at Endeavour Inlet or Punga Cove but they had been eliminated from consideration. None of them was in the right place. And, it could be argued, the features of the ketch described by Wallace were loosely similar to the general features of the *Blade*.

So any case against Watson would have to identify the *Blade* by excluding all the other possibilities and arguing that Wallace's description of a ketch could be discounted as a brief glimpse in bad light.

In early May Nicola Crutchley, of the Crown Law Office in Wellington, was invited to Blenheim to familiarise herself with the file and give a considered legal opinion about the strength of the Crown's case. If it went to trial, she would most likely be leading the Crown's case because she was the Crown solicitor for the Blenheim area. Following her visit there were weeks of discussion between police and Crutchley over Watson's arrest. Meanwhile, Pope and the Operation Tam team were coming under increasing media criticism about an inquiry that appeared to be heading nowhere. In reality, Pope was convinced he had a strong enough case to arrest Watson and lay charges. It was a question of convincing everyone else who was brought into the loop as police prepared to move.

One of the difficulties any trial would have to contend with would be the lack of bodies and the paucity of forensic evidence. The hair was still undergoing more sophisticated DNA testing, and who could predict what that might yield? Would it be best to arrest now on the basis of what the DNA had yielded so far, or would it be better to hope for a more conclusive result? Certainly, apart from the hair, much of the evidence against Watson was circumstantial, but circumstantial evidence had won many a case, police believed.

And police also knew they would have to deal with the problem caused by one witness, Don Anderson, who said he had taken a man who looked like Watson alone out to a boat at about 2 a.m. on New Year's morning. Any defence would be certain to argue that Anderson's evidence proved Watson had gone alone to the *Blade*, and so was off the scene and could not have been the man delivered by Guy Wallace on his water taxi with the young couple. But it was possible that Watson did in fact go out to *Blade* about 2 a.m. but then go back ashore, because there were plenty of witnesses who saw him at the Lodge after 2 a.m.

Police believed that the mountain of such facts produced by the inquiry, many of them apparently insignificant in themselves, added up to a comprehensive picture of Watson's guilt, despite lawyers' worries about how well the case would stack up. To the police, it was necessary to look at the evidence in totality, rather than quibble over individual aspects. And in this case, far more than most, there was huge media and public interest, so police were particularly keen to bring it to closure as soon as possible. Adding to the pressure was the fact that police believed, at this time, that Watson was about to run. They believed he was making plans to sail to Peru – and that would effectively end any prospect of bringing a successful prosecution against him. In their view, the time was right to move. An arrest now, they believed, would give them the opportunity to put key questions to Watson. They had vital information such as the near-identification of Olivia's hair to put to him. All along, police had thought it was highly improbable that Watson would confess to anything. But there was always a hope that if they could catch him offguard by revealing the strength of their case, his reaction could reveal even more. That opportunity would be lost if they delayed an arrest until after Watson's defence lawyers had been told about the results of the DNA testing.

To add to Pope's difficulties as winter closed in, a Parliamentary select committee began asking questions about Operation Tam. The MPs wanted a progress report on a case that, according to many reports in the media, was floundering, failing to make any tangible progress. The Commissioner of Police, Peter Doone, asked Pope to supply information to be provided to the select committee. Pope stressed the mountain of work that had been undertaken by Operation Tam.

'The operation inquiry base relocated from Blenheim to Christchurch on Friday, 29 May 1998. Current staffing complement is 10, inclusive of two Blenheim personnel. Ninety-five percent of the inquiry work has been completed with nearly 3600 witnesses interviewed, which includes over 1600 people present at Furneaux Lodge on New Year's Eve.

'As a result of intensive investigative work conducted over the past 4 months, substantial progress has been made in firming a reconstruction of the events leading to Smart and Hope's disappearance.

'It is quite clear that the couple have died as a result of foul play with the inquiry narrowing considerably as to criminal responsibility for their deaths. The focus of the investigation remains entirely committed to three central planks:

- Movements of Hope and Smart through the evening up to the time of their last known sighting on a 'boat'.
- Movements of a 'mystery' man through the evening, and last seen in the company of Hope and Smart on the 'boat'.
- Movements and sightings of the sloop which has been extensively canvassed in the media.

'Despite the huge and wide-ranging nature of inquiries, the investigation has crystallised to a very small number of issues which will impact on to the final resolution of this case.'

It was a very brief summary but Pope added a final paragraph to Doone which he did not want to be passed on to the select committee.

'The inquiry is now at a stage where sufficient facts have been obtained for a positive evaluation of criminal liability to be undertaken. This process is presently being conducted. (I expect a resolution to this matter!)' In other words, he wanted approval for action, very soon.

Finally, the decision came. Scott Watson would be arrested. Police responded quickly, and drew up plans for 'Operation Tam Crunch' – the co-ordinated sting execution that would on one day swing into place throughout the country to arrest Watson and, in the same fell swoop, attempt to gather the information which police believed they would have one chance to grab, provided they moved quickly enough. Operation Tam Crunch was carefully planned, down to the last detail and rationale. The plan, drawn up by Pope, began with an outline of the situation.

'On January 2 1998, Benjamin Innes Smart and Olivia Jane Hope were reported missing by their families after failing to return from New Year's Eve celebrations at Furneaux Lodge, Endeavour Inlet, situated in the Marlborough Sounds.

'An intensive police investigation has been conducted since that time in order to establish the circumstances of the missing couple's disappearance.

'It is inescapable that Smart and Hope have been murdered.

'Inquiries have recently focused on the activities and movements of Scott Watson and his criminal involvement regarding the deaths of Smart and Hope.

'There is sufficient evidence to arrest Watson for the murders of Smart and Hope.'

After outlining the situation, the plan for Operation Tam Crunch moved to the next phase, the execution. It would be a two-phase operation which would be carried out using arrest, search and interview groups. For phase one, one group in Rangiora, where Scott Watson was staying with his brother, would process Watson and carry out miscellaneous search duties. Another group in Picton would interview other members of the family and carry out searches, including ones of Watson's parents' home. Another group in Purau Bay, Lyttelton Harbour, would seize and search the *Blade*.

Then there would be phase two which would centre on interviewing a series of key witnesses who police had already talked to, but who they believed would have more to say if they believed Watson was going into custody. Another group was to be in action in the North Island to interview key witnesses. All the groups had to be prepared to cope with circumstances unforeseen in the plans. 'It may be assumed with some certainty that on or before termination date, one or more of the subjects to be interviewed will be in a different location to that specified. In this event, groups must accordingly be prepared to exercise some flexibility.'

Nevertheless, Pope issued detailed instructions for what he hoped would be a water-tight plan.

'This operation will terminate on Monday 15 June 1998, commencing at 0600 hrs.

'The officer in charge of group one will ascertain travel times and carefully plan his movements to ensure arrival at Watson's address at 0715 hrs on termination date.

'The officers in charge of all other groups shall *not* deploy to their respective group addresses until such time as Watson has been detained, and when directed to do so by O/C: Operation.

'All Blenheim group members will move into their respective areas on the mid-evening preceding termination day.

'Christchurch and Nelson members will travel to Blenheim in plain cars. Staff activities for the evening will be restricted to the respective motel accommodation and every effort made to ensure that the police presence is indistinct,' Pope ordered.

'Staff are to be mindful that in many instances occupants of properties to be searched have no obvious involvement in Watson's activities. Therefore discretion in terms of entry, securing and separation, needs to be exercised wisely.

'The officer in charge of each search is to carefully plan the search, fully brief staff on requirements, allocate search areas and record. He is to ensure that very thorough searches are conducted in accordance with standard requirements.'

Pope had an additional caution for his team.

'This operation has not progressed sufficiently to a point where every piece of evidence has been able to be obtained. Interviewing officers are not to assume that the operation has established all necessary evidence. Interviews are critical to the success of this operation. Accordingly, they must be conducted with a view to eliciting all possible information and establishing further evidence. A successful interview, not only of suspects but also of witnesses, may well establish further evidence.'

While the 'crunch' was to be carried out with maximum discretion, Pope warned that the news media, who had hounded Operation Tam all along, were certain to twig to what was happening.

'It is certain that operational activities on termination day will attract media attention. A planned strategy is in place to deal with the media. In the event of any inquiries from the news media, these are to be referred to the O/C Operation to ensure a co-ordinated response. Approaches to staff by media or other personnel in relation to this operation are to be met without comment and immediate referral to the O/C Operation.

'Under no circumstances are the news media to be advised of this operation. The O/C Operation is the only person authorised to make media comment.'

As for 'commands and signals', Pope himself would be in charge of the operation, and he would be based in Blenheim. The operation headquarters would be Level 12 of the Christchurch Central Police Station.

Finally there were certain practical details to take care of: police staff who qualified for a travelling allowance would have to buy their own meals. 'A meal allowance of $65.53 and an incidentals allowance of $8.05 can be drawn as an advance from accounts section, prior to departure.'

Telephonists at the Christchurch station were given their own warning: 'As a result of police activity in connection with Operation Tam scheduled for Monday 15 June and Tuesday 16 June 1998 there is likely to be extreme media interest and the Central Police Station can expect to take the majority of the telephone queries. Detective Inspector Pope will not be able to be contacted directly and all media inquiries are to be put to either the Operation Tam base or through to the media liaison officer . . . Calls for Detective Inspector Pope are not to be referred to his office number nor his cellphone.'

The crunch went largely according to plan, down to the intense media interest expected by police.

'Nearly six months after the South Island's biggest police inquiry began,' the Christchurch *Press* reported on 16 June, 'sloop owner Scott Watson has been charged with the murders of Ben Smart and Olivia Hope.

'Watson was arrested at dawn yesterday at his brother's house in Rangiora.

'He appeared in the Christchurch District Court yesterday charged with the murders of Benjamin Innes Smart, 21, and Olivia Jane Hope, 17, within the confines of the Marlborough Sounds and Cook Strait on January 1.

'The 26-year-old appeared in the dock for a matter of seconds, long enough for those in the packed courtroom to stare in silence at the man charged with one of the country's most shocking crimes.

'Watson, dressed in black jeans, red sweatshirt, and with a jacket covering his hands, showed no expression during his brief appearance.

'His lawyer, John Hardie, did not seek name suppression or bail. Judge Edward Ryan remanded Watson in custody to appear again on June 29.

'Outside the court, Mr Hardie said he did not seek name suppression as the arrest was all above board and Watson had no reason to be secretive. Although Watson has not entered a plea to the charges, Mr Hardie said Watson would maintain his innocence.

'Although Ben and Olivia's parents were not in court, other friends and relatives were there to witness Watson's appearance along with several of the detectives working on the inquiry and a huge media contingent. Watson's family was not present but some friends were.

'The head of the Operation Tam murder inquiry, Detective Inspector Rob Pope, travelled to Blenheim on Sunday night to tell the Hope and Smart families of the arrest and to prepare for yesterday's events. Inspector Pope was adamant that the arrest was not the end of the inquiry. He has always said the team would not be satisfied until they found the bodies of the young friends and brought them home.

'"This does not signal the end to the investigation as we have yet to locate Ben and Olivia," he said. "Inquiries will continue with the same focus and direction."

'Police have seized the sloop at the centre of the inquiry for a second time. The boat, which has been at Purau for several weeks, was hauled out of the water at Lyttelton early in the morning by police. It was trucked to a hangar at Wigram and will be held indefinitely. Several search warrants were carried out by police in Marlborough and Canterbury at the homes of Watson's brother, sister and parents.

'Watson was arrested after police swooped on his brother's house in Rangiora about 7 a.m. yesterday while the family was starting breakfast. Police searched the East Belt house before reportedly removing an item. Inspector Pope would not report if anything was removed.

'Watson's friends and family said they were shocked by the arrest. He had given them no expectation over the weekend that he expected to be arrested.

'Inspector Pope will spend today carrying out inquiries in Blenheim before returning to Christchurch tomorrow. He did not expect any further charges would be laid regarding the murders of Ben and Olivia.

'Watson was held at the town's police station for four hours before being taken to the Christchurch Central Police Station ready for his court appearance.

'More than 126,000 police man-hours and $3 million have been put into solving the disappearance of the two friends.'

Publicly, Watson's arrest was reported as a sort of closure for Pope and his team. After months of apparently little progress, media speculation about false leads and second-guessing of the police, public murmuring about the competence of Operation Tam, impatience and at times outright exasperation from the families of Ben and Olivia – expressed mainly by Gerald Hope – Pope at last had a trophy to present to the world.

He could drop his dogged 'No comment' replies to reporters, which had become virtually a daily ritual of Operation Tam. Pope said that in 23 years of policing he had never seen such intense and extended media interest in a case. And while police often court media interest, to flush out information or assuage public concerns, this time the reporters had gone way over the mark, he believed, trying to drive the inquiry rather than merely report it. Now, at last, Operation Tam had produced a result.

Nevertheless, the DNA evidence that had been at the centre of the legal argument over whether Watson should be arrested yet was still not in from Britain. It would be 1999 before anything like a definitive result came out of the laboratory.

In the meantime, the police and the prosecution lawyers had to face the huge task of getting the case ready to take Watson to trial.

II

IN COURT

IN LATE NOVEMBER 1998 THE Wither Hills on Blenheim's southern horizon were already parched brown in the heat. The Californian poppies were flowering brilliant orange in the riverbeds. The hot, dry days of summer had arrived already. It might have seemed as if the old rhythms of life had returned to Marlborough: another long hot summer was rolling around; another vintage of wine was swelling on the vine. 'The rain has stopped, the grass is still green and the tourists are starting to flock to Marlborough,' celebrated the local paper, the *Marlborough Express*. The big news in the paper was no longer the Ben and Olivia story but a heated controversy over an expensive new proposal for Blenheim, Stadium 2000. And one of the main players in that scrap was Gerald Hope, who had been elected mayor of Marlborough in the recent local body elections.

But last summer's story was about to descend on Blenheim again. The little District Court building was preparing to open its doors for Scott Watson's deposition hearings, the pre-trial determination of whether there appeared to be a substantial case against him. Despite the months of preparation – and the 1345 kilograms of police papers that were trucked up from Christchurch for the hearing – Ben's and Olivia's families were still uncertain about what to expect. Who would actually give evidence? Would they be cross-examined? Would they finally get to hear what had happened to their children? And on a personal level, how would they cope with sitting in the small courtroom a few metres away from the man who had apparently wrecked their lives?

'I just know that I'm very frightened of my emotions and anger towards him,' Mary Smart reflected. Among all four parents, she was the one who appeared to the public to have come the farthest in terms of dealing with the tragedy and getting on with something approaching a normal life. But she knew that her determination to rise above the situation could only go so far. 'I feel like killing the guy. I'm very, very, very angry, and if I saw him I don't know what I'd do. If I were the court authorities, I would actually search me before I went in there. I don't think I've ever felt such cold anger and hatred – I don't know, I wouldn't want to kill him. I'd just want to hit him so it hurt. But I couldn't do it unless I had a weapon.' And yet: 'I don't want to get bitter as a person. I'm not saying I don't want to get bitter towards Scott Watson. I don't want to make other people feel that I'm living in the past and being morbid over the loss of Ben. I don't want that to happen. Ben would never have wanted that to happen, would he?' she asked her husband, John.

He had other concerns – that the months of court procedures that were about to get under way might never, in the end, give them the news they so desperately wanted. They could come out of it none the wiser about what happened to Ben and Olivia.

'What concerns us is the court hearing is coming up and we may still never know what happened,' John said. 'Even when we go through a trial, we don't know if this guy's guilty or not. We have to take the police word for it. But even if he is, we still might not ever know what he did, or why.

'The police have been quite definite that he won't say anything about what happened, even if he's convicted.'

But there was no question about whether they would go along to the court.

'Yeah, we have to,' Mary said. 'You know something that's interesting – Jan said to me today, "I don't know how I'm going to go along there and sit there with his family." I said, "I've thought that too. But John said to me his family will be feeling much worse than we will." But she said to me, "I don't think they're the sort of people who will care." She said, "I'm scared they're going to be brazen and give us dirty looks all they way through." But they will care, won't they? They must.'

Though he never really doubted that the case against Watson was strong enough to go to trial, Rob Pope was concerned about just how well the evidence would play out. He believed police had compiled a compelling narrative that led to an overwhelming conclusion – that Watson was guilty. But he knew that it all hung, quite literally, on a thin strand.

'When you hear the evidence unfold in the sequence it should, you'll see quite a commonsense accumulation of Watson's activities and actions, along with Hope and Smart's. You're dealing with a huge range of activities in the early hours of New Year's Eve which narrows considerably up to 4 a.m., where you've only got half a dozen players. That's the whole purpose of the huge number of witnesses. To take it further, into the criminal arena, you still need to put Hope and Smart on the boat.'

Pope believed that despite Guy Wallace's insistence that he had taken the couple to a two-masted ketch, not a sloop, there were enough other witnesses to put Ben and Olivia on the water taxi with Watson and, from there, to conclude that the boat they had boarded must have been the *Blade*.

But Pope knew it wouldn't be enough merely to convince a future jury that the couple was last seen boarding Watson's boat.

'The trick will be proving the unlawful act. And on the face of it, the case may not seem strong, and it will come under rigorous attack.

'First off, we have to negate accidental death – one person on a boat possibly could have slipped off without knowledge. The probability of two people disappearing accidentally is certainly very remote; certainly two people who knew each other, who went to Furneaux independently, joined up for the night and were going to have a sleep, tired, taken in by a boatie, last seen there, yet within an hour that boat's disappeared. So, accidental? Highly unlikely in the circumstances.

'In terms of proving death has taken place, I think we can fairly prove that just through the lack of operation of bank accounts, all of the jobs that they were heading away to. They're neither depressed nor pessimistic sort of people. They both had appointments they didn't keep. She was looking forward to a job at Wairau Wines with Mum. Ben had a couple of band engagements and loved his music, all of that sort of stuff. So proving death shouldn't be a problem even though we haven't got the bodies.'

If the prosecution could prove that Ben and Olivia had died and that they had last been in Watson's company, it would still have to prove that Watson was responsible.

'That's where the forensic evidence comes into play. We've got a boat that's been meticulously cleaned down on all the contact surfaces.' The cleaning itself would be used to support the claim that Watson had tried to cover up something. The only fingerprints found inside the *Blade* were those of Watson himself and his sister, Sandy. Police would argue they showed she had helped him with the cleaning. But it was the forensic evidence that had been missed in the clean-up that would be crucial.

'Proving the unlawful act essentially relates to three bits of silent evidence – the fingerprints, the hatch cover with the scratch marks on it, and the hair.'

As the case went to depositions, Pope was still awaiting the results of the DNA testing in Britain. But he knew there was a strong 'probability' that the strands of hair found on the *Blade* were Olivia's.

'It's inescapable that her hair is on the boat. And the reasons for that no doubt will be attacked. But I would consider it very unlikely if the defence could actually attack the fact that it is her hair, because it is pretty solid and rigorous scientific evidence. How it got there is a different matter.

'But it is absolutely vital in terms of bringing the case. Without that we would be missing that vital cog in the wheel. There is some forensic evidence over and above the hair which supports the proposition that something nasty has gone on on that boat. But ultimately you've got the hair which somehow has got there.

'Really, it all comes down to the hair. Because that is the one incontrovertible, undeniable piece of silent evidence.'

Legal arguments dominated the depositions, at least for a start. The hearing was to have been presided over by two justices of the peace, but at the last minute Crown prosecutor Nicola Crutchley asked for the case to be heard before a judge. Chief District Court Judge Ron Young agreed to the request, citing the strong public interest in the case and the 'complex evidential material'.

Judge Peter McAloon was put in charge, and he immediately had a decision to make. Crutchley, intensely wary of all the media coverage the case had generated, took the highly unusual step of asking that the whole hearing be suppressed. Any more publicity about the case would risk tainting a future jury, she argued. The judge took only 30 minutes to deny the suppression order, but the Crown immediately went to the High Court in Wellington to lodge an appeal. That, too, failed, so the public would at last get to hear the outline of the Crown's case against Watson.

When proceedings got under way, interest centred on Watson himself. With short hair and wearing a suit, shirt and tie, he looked little like the demon who had haunted the story for almost a year. He sat impassively throughout the hearing, taking notes but showing few signs of emotion or interest in what was happening. His parents sat immediately behind him in the public gallery a couple of metres away from the Smart and Hope families and their supporters, on the other side of the courtroom's centre aisle.

TVNZ and TV3 of course sent reporters to cover the hearing and, with cameras barred from the courtroom, they filed regular reports from outside the courthouse. Most of New Zealand's other mainstream media were represented, with one or two media luminaries such as Barry Soper from IRN filling out the press bench. Yet most of the time it was a surprisingly low-key initial court outing for the case that had become the most publicised crime in recent New Zealand history.

The train of witnesses brought on by the Crown told a story that most of the country was already pretty familiar with, though now there were more details. Crutchley opened with a summary of the Crown case against Watson, but the witnesses were not always presented in any logical order, and it was frequently difficult to grasp the case the Crown had put together. And as Rob Pope was all too well aware, the DNA identification of the hair found on the *Blade* was still tentative at best. The buzz around the press bench was that police had a flimsy case against Watson.

Not surprisingly, scepticism about the case reached a new high when Guy Wallace took the stand. He had always been a potentially difficult witness, but police could hardly have expected the bombshell he delivered. He got through his initial evidence more or less satisfactorily; but then defence lawyer Mike Antunovic had a trap for him in cross-examination, and Wallace leapt right in. Wallace had described a scruffily dressed and unshaven man drinking alone in the Furneaux bar on New Year's Eve. He said it was this man whom he later ferried out to a boat, picking up Ben and Olivia on the way. This was the man police said was Scott Watson.

In front of the court, Antunovic showed Wallace a photo of Watson with a group of revellers. In the photo, Watson appeared clean-shaven and tidily dressed. Wallace readily identified Watson, but when Antunovic told him the photo was taken at about 10 p.m. on New Year's Eve, Wallace was astonished.

'Really?' he said. 'I find that very hard to believe.'

'Scott Watson couldn't have been the man you dropped off, could he?' Antunovic asked.

'I just find it very hard to believe it was taken at that time.'

'Just accept for the moment, if you will, that the photo was taken some hours before you dropped the couple off on the ketch.'

'Okay,' Wallace agreed.

'That is proved by other evidence in the case, and I believe it was some time around 10 or 10.30 p.m. on New Year's Eve.'

Wallace paused. 'If that's the case, it wasn't Scott Watson who I dropped off.'

There was a collective intake of air around the courtroom. It was one of those moments, common in courtroom dramas but rare in the real thing. Days of tedious evidence, not to mention months of investigation, had come to this. If you believed the reporters who rushed out to file their stories, the police case was in shreds.

Less surprisingly, Wallace went on to repeat his belief that he had taken the man, with Ben and Olivia, to a ketch, not a sloop as the police contended. He agreed when Antunovic suggested he must have been amused by the police's suggestion that Watson's sloop was the boat at which he had dropped off the three. 'I remember saying, what's going on here? It was not the boat I dropped them off on.'

When he left the court at the end of the day, Wallace was agitated. 'That really threw me, that photo,' he said to police. 'Did you see that photo? He looks clean-shaven.'

But Pope was being philosophical. 'That's not fatal. We can get around that,' he said later. Police had at least one witness who appeared in the same group photo and who also had a couple of days' growth. He appeared clean-shaven as well, so the photo was clearly deceptive, police argued. Watson's clean-shaven appearance must have been a trick of the flashlight. 'But that was lost on the media, in the great crusade to un-convict the convicted,' Pope said.

'We'd said to Wallace all along, "Don't worry about what they say, just stick to what you know." He said, "It was Watson on the boat. There's no way I'll forget those beady eyes of his."'

Nevertheless the Crown had played safe and not asked Wallace, or any other witness, to identify Watson in the dock. A denial, there and then in the courtroom, that the man in the dock was the stranger he had delivered to a boat would have been disastrous for the case. From the reverse angle, a positive dock identification in front of a jury at the real trial would be a great piece of courtroom drama. 'Identification is not a problem. I'm more than comfortable with that,' Pope said. 'We've got 70-odd witnesses who all in varying degrees provide corroborative identification all the way through the evening.' Dock identification is very rarely used because it is generally argued by a defence to be inherently unfair to the accused – there is only one person standing there in the dock, so the witness is likely to pick him or her. During the Watson trial, dock ID was never used.

Even if it hadn't been a great day for the police, it was only that – one day in a much bigger battle, Pope believed. 'I don't want to demean things but the depositions are only a provincial match, not the test match, which is a completely different set of circumstances. There are certain things which Wallace could have said more qualitatively, but that's the nature of any witness. They've all got their own degrees of intellect or ability to get their message across or understand questioning. It's pretty clear that he wasn't really listening.'

Wallace's performance in court had been the tip of an iceberg of ongoing difficulties the police had experienced with their star witness. He held the crucial link for them – getting Ben and Olivia on board the *Blade* with Watson – but all along he had insisted the boat wasn't the *Blade* and now he appeared to be suggesting the stranger wasn't Watson.

'That would give you a degree of insight into the difficulties we've had,' Pope said. 'Despite all the difficulties we've got in terms of credibility and reliability, the one thing he's always been consistent on is that the man he put on the boat was the man he picked up in the Naiad, who was the same man who was at the bar.' If necessary, police would just have to rely on other witnesses to make the link. If they said the man at the bar was Watson, then the stranger on the Naiad also had to be Watson, because Wallace insisted they were one and the same.

'I'll be very interested looking at it at the trial itself to see how the dynamics unfold,' Pope said. 'The whole trick is to keep it simple. Depositions are often messy and tacky. It didn't come out well. The media were confused.'

It was no surprise, however, that Watson was committed to trial.

After successive delays, it was June 1999 by the time the trial began in the Wellington High Court. It was going to be an endurance course, expected to last at least three months and to cost taxpayers about $5 million. Finding jurors who can put their ordinary lives on hold for such a marathon is always difficult, but from a pool of 50, 12 were selected – five women and seven men, all pakeha and mainly in their 30s. So as columnist Rosemary McLeod pointed out in the *Sunday Star*

Times, Watson's fate was to be determined by Europeans like himself, and mostly not too distant from himself in age.

'On 2 January Gerald Hope reported to the police that his daughter was missing,' said Nicola Crutchley, at last opening the case before a jury, more than 18 months after the disappearance of Ben and Olivia. The public gallery had been full for at least half an hour before day one of the trial got under way, but seats were reserved for three families. The Hopes and Smarts were on the left, the Watsons on the right – the same division as in the depositions at Blenheim, only with reversed places. Someone thought ahead to bring along peppermints, which they distributed to friends while they waited for the trial to start.

The portraits of former High Court judges had been covered with maps and photos of Endeavour Inlet and its surroundings, to which the lawyers would refer the jury again and again. Presiding over it all was Justice Heron, who had a low-key, no-nonsense style. He is one of the longest-standing High Court judges in New Zealand, and is held in high regard by lawyers from both the prosecution and defence – though defence lawyer Mike Antunovic was to develop an increasingly testy relationship with him as the trial wore on. But day one was concerned with more basic matters. Turn off your cellphones, he warned the public and the reporters, wary of this scourge of orderly proceedings. In the midst of it all, Scott Watson was brought up to the dock, looking surprisingly sharp in a suit and yellow shirt, not unlike Al Pacino in his *Dog Day Afternoon* days.

The media bench was packed for the most sensational trial of 1999. Extra press seats were improvised behind the dock. Television cameras would bring highlights of the trial to the nation every evening. Among the media, young TV reporters who had virtually made their name with the long-running Ben and Olivia case rubbed shoulders with old hands of court reporting such as Pat Plunket, of the *Dominion*, Wendy

Murdoch, of the *Evening Post*, and Radio New Zealand's Merle Nowland. The television networks and metropolitan newspapers invented logos to 'brand' their coverage, invariably featuring smiling photos of Ben and Olivia or idyllic images of the Marlborough Sounds in their pointers to the stories. Media stars such as Paul Holmes and TV3's newsreader John Campbell would drop in from time to time, along with a handful of dedicated strangers who settled in for the duration. Law students were also to come and go throughout the trial. Within days, however, the sheer, turgid detail of it all would wither the crowd down to hardy regulars.

On day one, however, Crutchley easily held the courtroom's attention, outlining the facts of the case she would present. She had a big story to tell. Although most of the reporters present and just about everybody else in the courtroom – especially the families and their supporters – had heard the outline of it many, many times before, they were eager for details. She had plenty of cards to play in her opening address and she tabled them slowly.

The Crown, she said, contended that Ben Smart and Olivia Hope died by foul play. 'It is the Crown's contention that Scott Watson is responsible for their deaths.' This was hardly news to anybody. But in order to prove murder, the Crown would need to exhibit an intent to kill on Watson's part. Revisiting the well-known territory of the sheer mass of people who had been interviewed to back up that contention, she said the Crown had some 480 witnesses to call. And she drew the jury's attention to one of her props, a map of the Marlborough Sounds. It was territory to which the court, and the jury, would return again and again in the weeks to come. 'You will get to know this very well.'

And then she had another prop to display, an English tourist's video of the scene at Furneaux Lodge on New Year's Eve. The images looked like any young kids' big night out –

crowds, heat, badly distorted music, a lot of drinking going on. But when the video froze on stills of Ben and Olivia, the courtroom's attention was riveted: two bright and attractive young people were doing nothing more than having a good night out. Whatever else was uncertain, one thing was clear. Their fun had ended in disaster. The court's job would be to determine why that had happened. Looking at the video image, the reality of the jury's task must have been brought home bluntly to them: they had not merely to apportion blame, but to root out an evil that seemed far more pervasive. Something awful had happened to a couple of kids who were merely having a good time. The *Evening Post* put it this way: in the time before everything went wrong, 'Summer love blossomed in idyllic surroundings'. And then it had been wiped out. It wasn't merely the cause of two deaths that the jury were supposed to solve, but the reason why evil could stalk so horrifically, so randomly, in such a beautiful place. The question hovered behind the parade of witnesses brought to the High Court, each with a meticulously small part of the Crown's case to add.

By the end of the first week the trial had settled into something of a routine. The respective families – the Hopes, the Smarts and the Watsons – had settled into permanent places in the public gallery, and the jury and reporters were getting accustomed, in a second-hand sort of way, to the life of the Marlborough Sounds at holiday time. An awful moment had been frozen in time and it seemed that, for weeks and weeks on end, all the participants would be hauled into the courtroom to give their particular take on the circumstances.

'Imagine a long trial like this as one of those pointillist paintings made up of thousands of tiny dots,' columnist Rosemary McLeod wrote in the *Sunday Star Times* at the end of the first week. 'Right now, the evidence being heard is a bit like seeing the dots, but with little idea of what the whole picture will look like.'

The second week of the trial brought a relief from the parade of witnesses. The jury, along with media, lawyers and court officials, were flown to the Marlborough Sounds to get a first-hand feel of the place. Most of all, Pope and the prosecution team wanted them to see for themselves Scott Watson's boat. Whenever he had visited the *Blade*, Pope felt its claustrophobic interior was like a 'floating coffin', he said. As well as seeing the precise location of key exhibits such as the scratched hatch cover, Pope hoped the jury would get a feel for that too.

Like tourists on a nostalgia-themed outing, the jury and their attendants were flown from Wellington to the Sounds on a noisy old DC-3. It had been planned to make low passes over Furneaux Lodge and other key locations in the Sounds so the jury could get a feel of the geography, but on the day the wind was too high. In Marlborough they visited Shakespeare Bay and Waikawa Bay where Watson had moored the *Blade*. On the following day, when they visited Furneaux Lodge, the *Blade* and other about 14 other boats including the *Mina Cornelia* were moored at the sites they had occupied on New Year's Eve. There was no attempt to re-enact the key players' movements on New Year's Day morning, but the prosecution went to a lot of effort to help the jurors put themselves in the scene. In Endeavour Inlet they were ferried to the *Blade* and other boats on Naiad inflatables like the one that allegedly took Watson and the young couple to the *Blade* in the early hours of the morning. It was broad daylight on a frosty winter day rather than high summer in the Sounds, but still a very subdued mood hung over the party. That night, the judge, jury and prosecution lawyers spent the night at Punga Cove while the defence lawyers, several media and a group of police slept at Furneaux Lodge. In the morning they travelled across to Erie Bay, where Watson took the *Blade* on New Year's morning.

Then it was back to the routine of the courtroom for more weeks of witnesses, most of them boaties who had been in

Endeavour Inlet that night. Many reporters noted how attentive the jury remained throughout it all. Veteran reporter Frank Haden recorded in the *Sunday Star Times* how the jurors had sat through the testimony of hundreds of witnesses, all saying pretty well the same thing about events on the night of 31 December 1997 and, significantly, the early hours of 1 January. 'Already the jurors have taken aboard a mountain of detailed information, most of it repetition to the point of boredom, and they are only a quarter of the way through one of the most difficult trials imaginable.'

The prosecution was not merely filling time. It was attempting to establish where Ben and Olivia had gone through the only means possible: exclusion. 'The prosecution is still calling evidence from everyone who had a boat in the bay to establish that Olivia and Ben didn't spend the night on board,' Haden noted. 'Every boat except one. If 121 boats can be eliminated, the jury will be asked to accept that the doomed pair was on the only one left, Number 122,' which was the *Blade.*

Then the trial settled into a long series of witnesses who had stories to tell of Watson's 'sleazy', 'drunken' and 'offensive' behaviour on the night. Most pointedly, they were asked to recall his various chat-up lines to young women. One witness remembered how Watson had asked her to crew on his boat on a trip to Tonga. When she asked him the name of the boat, he replied, 'Anything you want it to be, sugar.' She had been flown in from Sydney to give that evidence. Others told their stories via a video satellite link to London.

By late July the trial was at its expected midway point, and Rosemary McLeod wrote that all the separate points of evidence had only just begun to converge into 'a fuzzy outline of possibility'.

'Many murder trials have a clear and obvious story from beginning to end,' McLeod wrote. 'Such clarity is not possible where, as in this case, no bodies have been recovered and there are no witnesses to the violence that may have occurred.' Everybody remarked how stone-faced Watson remained throughout it all. 'I saw him yawn last week which, as his demeanour goes, was a moment of high drama,' wrote McLeod.

Watson was not the only one yawning as the weeks wore on. At the Café Libretto, downstairs in the High Court building, reporters filled the breaks speculating about just *what* the Crown was attempting to prove with various witnesses. Despite a rumour – as unsubstantiated as most of the others that surrounded the case – that one juror had told somebody that Watson was 'as guilty as sin', few of the reporters were taking bets on the outcome. It was just too hard to tell. Pamela Stirling, writing for the *Listener*, was privately forming the view that the way things were going, if Watson didn't give evidence, the most likely outcome would be a hung jury. That had been the outcome of other celebrated long trials, such as the John Barlow and Vicky Calder cases. The press photographers rostered in shifts to cover the witnesses complained that it was the most boring job they could remember.

But nobody was yawning on 29 July. The courtroom was full, and that was a sight the reporters hadn't seen since the early days of the trial. Guy Wallace, the water taxi driver, was about to give evidence. He had caused huge excitement at the depositions with his failure to identify Watson from a photograph taken on the night. Would he identify Watson this time? And would he still insist he had taken the young couple and the man to a two-masted ketch, not Watson's sloop? High drama was expected. Some regulars went so far as to note that Crown prosecutor Nicola Crutchley had even changed her hairstyle for the big day, going for a plait instead of the normal roll arrangement.

Despite all the previous publicity he had generated as a very media-friendly star witness, Wallace infuriated the reporters and the TV networks by claiming protection from being pictured in court. Any witness had the right to seek such protection, but the reporters felt it was a bit rich from someone who had, they thought, courted so much publicity earlier.

In the event, Wallace immediately settled the prosecution's nerves by agreeing that the man in the picture could, after all, be Watson. He still thought the man did not have as much stubble as he remembered, but he had a reason for his earlier failure to identify the man in the photo as Watson. The man had his eyes closed, Wallace said, and the eyes were vital in recognising anyone's face. Watson, he said, had particularly 'mistrusting' eyes.

If that was a relief, Wallace was offering no solace on the boat question. He insisted he had taken the pair to a double-masted ketch with a blue stripe. He said he had seen television footage of Watson's sloop, the *Blade*, being lifted out of the water by police, and Crown prosecutor Paul Davison asked him if there were any similarities between the two boats. He said there was none. The boat on television was too short and it had only one mast. 'About the only similarity is that it floats,' he said.

The Crown called the owners of the all the ketches they could locate in the Marlborough Sounds over New Year to account for their movements and exclude them as Wallace's remembered boat. But at least one witness, Ted Walsh, maintained that he had seen a ketch two days after New Year, and police had never been able to account for it. He maintained he had seen the ketch while out on a fishing trip on his charter yacht, *Sweet Release*. One of the witnesses on that trip was a minor celebrity, All Black prop Greg Feek, and he brought the trial a moment of relaxation.

'Make sure you deal to those Aussies,' court cryer John Conoly muttered to Feek before making the usual request for the witness to swear to tell the truth in the evidence he was about to give. Feek had a tantalising memory of seeing a person with what looked like long blonde hair on board the ketch. 'It was like a girl's hair, long and wavy,' he said. But was the boat really a ketch? Feek couldn't remember if it had one mast or two. And anyway, he said, he didn't know much about boats and he had been more interested in fishing at the time. 'The blue cod were almost jumping into the boat,' he said.

The discrepancy between Watson's sloop and Wallace's memory of a ketch was left hanging unresolved. The best the police could manage remained the old strategy of elimination. Detective Bruce McLachlan was called in to tell the court that he had collected videotapes and photos from 280 people who had been at Furneaux. From them, he had clearly identified 176 boats in the inlet. Not one of them matched the ketch described by Guy Wallace.

So the trial moved to new territory: chiefly the early hours of New Year's morning and various sightings of a boat like the *Blade* 'wallowing', for instance, in one of the deepest parts of the Sounds at the entrance to Tory Channel, or stalled in a cove near Marine Head with a man crouching down near the stern apparently looking into the water.

Then there was the hair, and days of complex forensic evidence arguing that the hair found on the *Blade* was 28,000 times more likely to have come from Olivia than from any other unrelated female. The DNA testing carried out in Australia and Britain was also brought to court and was said to strengthen the likelihood that the hair was Olivia's. But the DNA testing could not offer a definitive positive result – an inevitable gap in such procedures and one which the defence inevitably questioned, along with questions about why there was a small hole in a bag containing the hair sample. In common with many cases of DNA identification, it was impossible to tell whether the jury was more swayed by the prosecution's mathematical probabilities or the defence's questions.

Confused, incomplete and sometimes inconsistent, the Scott Watson trial was painfully, slowly, joining up all the points of the picture. And despite all the detail that was amassing, it was not a markedly different picture from the one the public had gleaned many months ago, a long time before the trial began. On the press benches, opinion was solidifying, but only just. Pamela Stirling was coming round to the belief that Watson might be convicted. Merle Nowland was sure he was guilty. But, the sceptics said, Merle always had a tendency to believe the prosecution.

But more than 10 weeks in, the trial was at last about to deliver a bombshell. The Crown had decided on the risky tactic of delivering up two secret witnesses, prison informants who had met Watson in prison on remand, and they had conversations to relate. Earlier, Pope had been candid about the risks of using such informants. 'It's a two-edged sword,' he had said. 'But we would use it if we had something definitive.' By now, police had evidently decided the testimony of two prisoners was definitive enough.

After a raft of instructions from Justice Heron about what could and could not be photographed and reported, and with paper taped over the windows in the courtroom door to protect the identity of the witnesses, they were delivered to tell their story. As Pope puts it now, their appearance in the courtroom created an 'atmosphere you could cut with a knife. For the first time in the trial, we got away from white middle-class New Zealanders. They gave us a glimpse of the real Scott Watson.'

Witness A had shared a cell with Watson in Christchurch's Addington Prison. They had become friends after Watson had got into an argument with a gang member in which the witness had sided with Watson. They also shared a resentment of the prison guards. They had allegedly been hassling Watson by shaking him awake each morning, so, to put a stop to that, the two inmates had swapped beds.

The witness remembered how twice in the cell, he had been

'freaked out' by hearing Watson screaming in his sleep. The first time it happened, the witness kicked Watson awake and asked him if he was being haunted. Watson said no, but when it happened again and the prisoner asked Watson if 'those people' were haunting him, Watson said, 'Yeah, mate.' He took that as an indication that Watson had killed the pair and was having bad dreams.

'I said, "How the fuck can you fuck somebody when they're screaming?" He said, "They've got nothing on me."' The witness said he had broached the subject a couple more times later. Once, when they were doing press-ups together in their cell, he said Watson had showed him how he killed the couple. Watson had grabbed the prisoner by his jersey and pushed him against the wall, forcing his knee between the prisoner's knees, showing 'how he pulled her down. He said the bitch kept on kicking and punching.' When prosecutor Kieran Raftery asked the witness if Watson had said how he had overpowered Olivia, Watson had gestured to indicate 'a strangulation kind of thing'.

The inmate said that when he had asked Watson where the bodies were, Watson had only said that they wouldn't be found.

'I just looked at him as a different person,' the prisoner said. It was the last time they talked about the murders.

Witness B had been no friend of Watson's to start with. He was a gang member – the name of the gang was suppressed – and he had taken a dislike to Watson after they had an altercation in Addington Prison's weight room which had led to the equipment being confiscated. However, they had become mates and when Watson was being harassed by Black Power inmates because of his alleged crime, Witness B 'made it known that I was going to back Scott up if there was going to be any trouble'.

After that, the three of them – Watson, Witness A and Witness B – had taken to having conversations through the peephole in Watson's cell door, which they kept jammed open with a toothbrush. During one conversation they were joking about the murders of Ben and Olivia, and Witness B asked Watson if he had done it.

'You know I can't tell you that,' Watson said. 'I'm still having wet dreams about it.'

Once when Witness B said he wished he could see Watson's thoughts, like on a video, Watson replied that he 'would have a fuckin' good time'.

Another time the three of them were exercising in the prison yard. Watson popped a few Valium tablets that a visitor had brought in, and they talked about their personal problems. Crown prosecutor Paul Davison asked the witness if Watson had said anything, and the witness replied: 'He says – I don't know the exact wording – but he admitted to killing Ben Smart and Olivia Hope and he said, "They have got jack shit on me." I believed him. I physically blocked my ears and said, "I don't want to know."'

When they talked about where he had dumped the bodies, Watson indicated locations in the Marlborough Sounds and talked about 'sea lice', 'deep water' and 'virtually Cook Strait'. Later he said he dumped the bodies in an area of water containing volcanic silt which 'goes down endlessly'.

Another time, Witness B said, they were reading a newspaper story in which a psychic suggested one of the murder victims had been hit over the head. 'That's not how it was done,' Watson said. 'That's not how it was done.'

Watson told his mate that if he went down for the murders, then he, Witness B, should get a lawyer to protect him and help sell the story to the media. Watson reckoned the witness could make $3 million from the story which he would want a cut of.

As Pope said, prison informants are a high-risk strategy, and in cross-examination, defence lawyer Mike Antunovic wasted no time trying to discredit Witness B's background and motives.

'I don't believe in hurting innocent people, women and children especially – killing them,' the witness explained.

Antunovic spent more than 30 minutes detailing the witness's long criminal record; its details were suppressed, but included assaults on women and young people when he was young. The witness conceded to Antunovic that he had made his statement to police on the morning he was to appear for a depositions hearing on a serious violence charge. When he appeared, the charge was withdrawn and replaced with a less serious one, to which he pleaded guilty. Antunovic smelt a sort of plea bargain in return for the witness's story.

'Do you think it had anything to do with the police?' he asked.

'Nothing at all,' Witness B replied.

He agreed that police had provided him with a cellphone and a car since his release. And after tripping him up on the detail of who had supplied the Valium in the exercise yard, Antunovic accused him of making up the story of Watson's admission.

'Well, there was two of us that heard it,' Witness B replied. 'So . . . you know. He told me, eh. Don't sit there telling me he didn't.'

And after a few more witnesses – including Watson's girlfriend who said he had told her he hadn't done it – the Crown's case was at last over. They were yet to hear the summing up which would try to make sense of it all, but the jury had heard all the information the Crown could gather to prove that Scott Watson was guilty.

At the end of August the defence was finally to mount its case on Watson's behalf. They hoped they had already sowed the seeds of doubt through their cross-examination of Crown witnesses, and the defence itself would be very brief. The Crown had spent 11 weeks calling nearly 500 witnesses before the court, but the defence would take only about three days, with some 25 witnesses.

Mike Antunovic, opening the case, said that despite the volume of the Crown's evidence, the defence case was that it had been selective in the witnesses and the information it had presented. He did not attempt to undermine the gravity of the case. 'It was one of the major events that happens in our country, that affects all New Zealanders one way or another,' he said. Nor did he try to suggest that Watson emerged lily-white in the evidence. There were aspects of his behaviour at the New Year's Eve party 'that he will not be very proud of'. But how did his behaviour relate to the one crucial fact the Crown would have to prove: was Watson the mystery man on the water taxi that night?

'Their evidence tells us clearly that the mystery man cannot possibly be Scott Watson, and the vessel Olivia Hope and Ben Smart were seen to board cannot possibly be Scott Watson's boat.'

Not surprisingly, much of the defence's case revolved around trying to prove the existence of the as yet unaccounted-for ketch that Guy Wallace claimed to have taken Ben and Olivia to. Witnesses included a policeman who had seen a ketch with a blue stripe around its hull travelling under power off the west coast of the North Island in January 1998. Another woman had seen a ketch at about 7.30 a.m. on New Year's Day, heading out of Endeavour Inlet into Queen Charlotte Sound. And another witness had seen a ketch at about midday on New Year's Day sailing off Point Jackson where Queen Charlotte Sound opens into Cook Strait.

Scott Watson did not elect to give evidence; the right to remain silent is a fundamental right of any accused and, even if it may seem to imply to an outsider that the defendant has something to hide, jurors are always told by judges to read nothing into it. The jury had been deprived of hearing Watson's story tested in court, Justice Heron would say in his summing up. 'The one thing you must not do is assume he is guilty just because he has not gone into the witness box.'

So, on the first day of spring 1999, the defence case was all wrapped up. The judge, the lawyers for the Crown and the lawyers for the defence, and finally Justice Heron, would sum up, and then the whole long story would be in the hands of the jury to decide.

Paul Davison summed up for the prosecution, and his message to the jury was essentially simple: so much evidence pointed to Scott Watson as the culprit that the jury 'better look pretty closely at him'. He spoke to the court for an entire day and then a couple of hours the next morning with that message. When he was not dwelling on the evidence pointing to Watson, he was attempting to discredit the evidence that seemed to clear him. The biggest single factor there, of course, was the ketch Guy Wallace claimed to have taken the three people to. On that count, Davison said, the most remarkable fact was that not even Watson himself had claimed in his interviews with police to have seen a ketch.

Davison contended that the Crown's lack of much concrete evidence was in itself telling. 'The fact that the police could not find much evidence speaks volumes for the care with which the killer cleaned up after his act.' The absence of evidence also counted another way, he said: it excluded all the possibilities except Watson as the cause of Ben and Olivia's disappearance.

But to many the most interesting element in Davison's summing up was his concession, for the first time in the three-month trial, that Watson must have returned alone from Furneaux Lodge to the *Blade* at about 3.30 a.m. on New Year's morning – but that he later returned to the Lodge and then set about the events that had been the focus all along. The admission that he had made an earlier water taxi ride to the *Blade* allowed the jury to make sense of the evidence of water taxi driver Donald Anderson who had claimed to have dropped Watson alone at the *Blade* at about 3.30 a.m.

Bring your overnight gear tomorrow, Justice Heron told the jury when Davison was finished, just in case progress the next day was rapid enough to allow them to retire and consider their verdict.

When it was his turn to sum up, defence lawyer Bruce Davidson said the Crown's evidence was not merely 'pitifully weak' but in fact proved that Watson didn't do it. To back that up, he pointed to Wallace's ketch and to the Crown's admission of Watson's lone water taxi ride. He took much less time than his Crown counterpart to sum up, and then it was time for the judge to have his say.

'Nobody is in a better position than you are, having heard all the evidence,' Justice Heron told the jurors, pressing home the standard warning that the jurors make their decision purely on what they had heard in court, not on any other information or rumours they may have come across. His four-hour summing up kept the jury in court until after 9.30 p.m. and went over what he saw as the salient points of law in the Crown and defence cases. And he had something of a plea for the 12 jurors: to 'bring this dreadful act in the life of our country to finality'. Please, he said in so many words, reach a verdict, and do not leave this case hanging in the balance.

On Saturday 11 September the world was watching terror unfold in East Timor, and in Auckland the New Zealand government was hosting President Bill Clinton and the other leaders of APEC. But most of the country was waiting for one piece of news.

It was just after midday when the jury returned to court with their verdict. They had deliberated for 22 hours, spread over three days. As verdicts must be in New Zealand, their decision was unanimous: guilty.

Scott Watson had two words of his own before he was sent away to await sentencing: 'You're wrong.'

On 26 November 1999 Scott Watson was sentenced by Justice Heron to serve at least 17 years in prison.

'This is a bloody farce, I'm an innocent man,' Watson said as he was led from the courtroom. His brother Tom and mother Beverley also yelled abuse as they left the court, after hearing the minimum non-parole period. Crown prosecutor Nicola Crutchley had asked for a 14-year minimum sentence before Watson could be considered for parole, instead of the normal 10 years. But describing the murders as having 'the hallmarks of a lone psychopath', Justice Heron gave Watson a minimum prison term of precisely the same number of years Olivia Hope had lived before meeting her death on New Year's morning.

Bruce Davidson said Watson maintained his innocence. His family, he said, would 'fight as long as there is breath in their bodies'.

Immediately after his guilty verdict, Scott Watson's lawyers said they planned to appeal. They had several months to prepare their case before the Court of Appeal. From the start, they were coy about the grounds they would appeal on, only saying there was reason to argue the conviction was 'unfair'.

In early 2000 there were rumours around Marlborough that the defence lawyers had sent private investigators back into the field to try to gather new evidence. But the appeal would have to hang on points of law raised in the initial case, and it was unlikely the points of law would be wide enough to allow anything like a full scale re-litigation of the case.

The Crown was to learn the precise grounds for the appeal in late March, in time to prepare to go back to the Court of Appeal in mid-April 2000.

In late November 1999 Scott Watson was sentenced for some minor charges that had come to light during the Operation Tam inquiry: principally, the stealing of a $400 aluminium dinghy while in Whangarei on the *Blade* in November 1997. He had originally been detained on the charge before being charged with the murders of Ben and Olivia. He had pleaded guilty.

Watson had also pleaded guilty to assaulting a policeman and to damaging his police cell during his detention in the Blenheim Police Station for the depositions hearing. A charge that he had an offensive weapon, a 7-centimetre piece of steel from the handbasin frame in his cell, was withdrawn. The charge at last shed some light on the bruise that had been visible on his face during the depositions, the result of a scrap in the cells. The matter had been suppressed at the time. When police had tried to remove him from his cell after finding him smoking, he had head-butted Sergeant Peter Reed, injuring his cheek.

Justice Marion Frater said the charges were minor, and could be dealt with by a two-month sentence added to his life term. Originally, however, she forgot to mention a just-passed requirement that home detention could be considered as an alternative to short jail sentences. She called Watson back into the Wellington District Court to go through the motions of advising the guilty man of the possibility of home detention.

'That would be nice,' defence lawyer Bruce Davidson said, rolling his eyes to the ceiling.

12

UNENDING

DAVID BAKER HAS A LOT OF MEMORIES of Operation Tam, mainly from the weeks he spent as a volunteer with the Marlborough Coastguard helping police with the searching. But as a professional paua diver working the Sounds, he's constantly out in the waters where Ben and Olivia disappeared.

'It was awful to start with because we were on edge. I think it was probably in February, we were diving in Wellington Bay, which is one of the drift areas that is a possibility if he had chucked them over the side. I got dragged out in a bit of a swell down over a sort of a gut and down onto some bones. Of course I was thinking, What is this? But it was a poor dead seal. Yeah, there's not a day I don't think about it when I'm on the water now, the whole year. Because you just think maybe there's something still out there to be found. I mean, it would be good to find something just to say to those kids' parents, Well, look, we know where they went.

'But I don't think we probably will now, after this time. We've dived all the coast, all the places they could have possibly been. It sticks with you. I know we used to talk about coming home when you're tired and just thinking about how those mums and dads would be feeling. There are times when I've been working with my son and I know what it is like to worry. I've lost my boy a couple of times diving, when something's gone wrong and we've been separated. I have a bit of fatherly panic before I find him. Hell, it's nothing compared to what they've been through, but I know what the feeling's like. I think about it all the time. I think we all do. Not as much as we did, of course, but we still do.

'I guess it made worldwide news. Of course, overseas there's so many bloody murders and things all the time. But around here it's made people aware that the place isn't quite as nice and secure as it was, that's for sure. It's certainly made all the parents a bit more thoughtful about what's happening.'

The case may have reminded locals that evil could stalk the idyllic the Marlborough Sounds, but ironically Operation Tam was credited with bringing about a 5.75 percent drop in reported crime in the Marlborough district in the year to June 1998. Police put that down to all the uniforms in the district for Operation Tam. Criminals could have got the idea that there were police in every second car on the roads, said the Tasman district manager, Superintendent Barry Davies. The biggest reduction was for crimes of violence and drugs. But there was a further irony. Sexual offences were up by 13.1 percent.

In the early summer of 1998–99, as Marlborough prepared to mark the first anniversary of Ben's and Olivia's disappearance, the province launched a new 'identity'. A public relations company was contracted to develop a new brand for Marlborough, that would capture the heart of old Marlborough and embrace the essence of the new, much more trendy province of wineries, olive groves and gourmet foods. On a beautiful balmy evening 200 or 300 locals gathered in Blenheim to see the results of the PR exercise and find out how Marlborough was to present itself to the rest of New Zealand and – given the booming exports of products such as wine and mussels – the world. One of the speakers was Gerald Hope, who, since New Year 1998, had become mayor of the Marlborough District Council. The anchor for the evening was Tessa Nicholson, the *Marlborough Express* reporter who had led the paper's reporting of the disappearance of Ben and Olivia.

The new brand, the crowd was told, was all about 'who we are and what we can become'. It was about associating Marlborough with a set of 'aspirational objectives'. It had to distil the essence of the place and establish the 'psychic premium' of Marlborough. The cluster of ideas that the brand had to represent, the PR people said, had to be both traditional and forward-looking. So it was rooted in an idea of Marlborough that all the locals there that night could readily identify with. 'Our remoteness builds strong people and strong families,' the audience was told. 'Kids who grew up in Marlborough were allowed to be kids.' The province, they were told, had to develop not just a new brand, but a new attitude, taking the heart of what was best from the past but looking at it anew. So the core of the new identity had to look young. Marlborough had to realise that all those old values it had been jealously guarding for years as a secret it didn't really want outsiders to share were really tremendous assets. In a world looking for values and quality lifestyles, old Marlborough could be re-styled as a haven associated with all the good things in life. Far from being a backwater that anyone with ideas and ambition left as soon as they were old enough, it could be a magnet for people wanting a decent life *and* cutting-edge, high-quality sophistication. It could be a sort of paradise with attitude.

'That's what will bring the kids back. They get out and do the city hassle thing, and then they realise their heart is here.' The psychic premium of Marlborough would be summed up in a brand that would be carried on wine bottles, tourism promotions and anything else that the province presented to the outside world: 'Love Marlborough,' with the M of Marlborough drawn as a heart, wrapping the brand in love. It was supported on the screen by a stunning image of a boy, a girl and the water of a sheltered bay. Was there anyone in the audience that night who didn't see in the image an echo of Ben and Olivia, two fine young Marlborough kids who were about to take on life in the outside world, two kids whose hearts would forever be in Marlborough?

Woodbourne Air Force base, up the Wairau Valley from Blenheim, has always been a bit apart from the rest of Marlborough, both the old province of farming families and small-town life and the newer Marlborough of wineries, olive groves and cafes. To Squadron Leader Rob van Lent, the weeks the Air Force spent supplying volunteers to search for Ben and Olivia helped to bridge that gap.

'There's a perception, I guess, that we've got all these young blokes here on the base charged up with hormones who head off into town and chat up the local ladies more readily than the locals get to. There's a bit of animosity about that. So we've worked very hard at pushing the fact we believe that we're part of the Marlborough community. That was a big thing during the investigation. I tried to push it that people didn't look upon us as being the military and outsiders in this. This is a community response to a community problem, and all the people on base are very much of that ilk. I remember saying to somebody in a press interview one time that for the younger people I think they can identify very closely with the two kids who had gone missing. For those of us that are a bit older and greyer, we can identify with the plight of the parents, of just not knowing where your kids are. That wasn't anything to do with whether you're Air Force, a plumber or a grass cutter. That's a human instinct, and the response was a human response. When we put the word round for volunteers for the searches we were just overwhelmed.'

The way priests often are, Father Barry Scannell was shifted from Blenheim in the early days of the investigation. He hated going, after having become close to John and Mary Smart. But he kept in close touch with them from his new parish in Auckland. He was with them in court when Scott Watson's guilty verdict was read. He also watched the change that the case brought to the town that had been his home for a few years.

'A place like Marlborough, a place like Blenheim, could never be the same after an incident like that, especially when it was not someone from outside the region who was the accused. I personally feel that the locals have actually shown quite a bit of restraint. A place like Marlborough is very conservative, people have fairly fixed ideas, it is not a place that embraces multi-culturalism in a big way. If it had been someone who was a tourist passing through or someone from out of the region, many people might have found it easier to accept. I mean, it is only in the last year or so that they had their first armed hold-up. They have had two or three since then, but I think that the underworld side of this case was a real eye-opener for a lot of people.

'In recent years a tremendous number of new people have come into Marlborough. It had been very established there for generations, but with the wine industry, the mussel industry and a few more things happening around Marlborough, more people have come in, and that really has changed the traditional way people see things around there. The thriving dope industry was a tremendous revelation to all the people of Marlborough – well, to most of them. Most people in Blenheim had never really associated with the sorts of people this case threw up. I think the town can never really go back to what it was after something like this has happened.'

John and Mary Smart and Gerald and Jan Hope came to know the media intimately in the first weeks of Operation Tam. They hoped that by speaking publicly, however much they hated it, something or someone might come forward with information about Ben and Olivia. As a result, the families became nationally recognised figures. Now they are trying to get back normal, anonymous lives. Bluntly, there's no reason to talk to the media any more. 'We did it for a reason,' Mary says. 'But Ben and Olivia are dead and there's no reason to do it now.'

'The hardest thing of the lot is not having the kids to bury properly. Is it possible that we can get them back now?' wondered a friend of John and Mary Smart and Gerald and Jan Hope. 'Watson's convicted now. He's away for the next 14 years or so. Can't he just give them that?'

The guilty verdict at the end of Scott Watson's trial was one form of closure for Ben's and Olivia's families. But they ache for more. Finding the bodies of their children would perhaps shed some light on exactly how they died and, just as importantly, allow the families to say a proper goodbye to Ben and Olivia.

A week after the trial ended, the Hopes and Smarts spoke to the *New Zealand Woman's Weekly* to ask that last unanswered question. 'John and I aren't naïve in terms of the logistics of finding the kids but it's not impossible and it's something which has to be monitored,' Gerald Hope told the *Woman's Weekly*.

But neither the police nor the Marlborough Sounds boaties, nor any of the friends who helped with searches hold out much hope of finding the bodies. In fact, many believe that for a long time there has been nothing left to find. 'The sea lice finish off anything pretty quickly,' a fisherman says. 'It just depends. Some parts of the Sounds aren't as bad, but at certain times of the moon – a new moon as it was then – they are very, very bad. Like if you leave a net overnight in the water with the fish in it, the fish will just be skin and bone in the morning, and that's decent-sized fish. Human flesh is pretty soft. I mean, I haven't had much to do with bodies being in overnight before, but I would imagine that in a couple of days there would be nothing much left, in most areas.'

Since the early days of the inquiry, police believed the bodies were probably in deep water at sea. The sightings of Watson's boat heading up Tory Channel to Cook Strait led them to believe that was where he had most likely dumped them. The searches of both possible locations, at the mouth of Endeavour Inlet and Erie Bay, had all but excluded those areas as possible sites. The deep waters of the strait and its fierce tidal movements meant there was virtually no chance of finding any bodies that had been dumped there.

Scott Watson could end the mystery – if his guilty verdict was correct. But his appeal of the conviction at the very least delayed the day when he might give the families of Ben and Olivia the past piece of information they wanted.

Some friends and others who had watched the trial held out some hope, however, that he might eventually talk. They listened particularly to the evidence that he was having nightmares in prison, which they took as a sign that he is not a psychopath. Instead, there must be a conscience behind the expressionless front he presented in court. If Watson's conscience troubled him enough to cause nightmares, he might eventually want to get something off his chest.

The cost of bringing Scott Watson to trial for the murders of Ben Smart and Olivia Hope has topped $5.7 million. Watson's legal aid bill alone is expected to be more than $700,000 – the most expensive in New Zealand's history. Watson's lawyers, Bruce Davidson and Mike Antunovic, were paid the top legal aid rate of $180 an hour for their services. The prosecution lawyers – Nicola Crutchley, Kieran Raftery, Mark Davies and Paul Davison QC, who joined the case as it prepared to go to the High Court – were expected to incur a total bill of around $400,000. The police's own costs were calculated to be in excess of $4 million when all the man-hours were added up. Included in the police estimate was about $100,000 for the forensic tests carried out in Britain. The added costs of taking the case to the Court of Appeal are yet to come in, but look likely to take the total bill beyond the $5.7 million estimate.

Still the unidentified mystery ketch that Guy Wallace insisted he delivered Ben and Olivia to continued to sail into history, long after the police search had failed to find it. In mid-February 2000 four men came forward to say they had seen a blue and white double-masted boat moored close to shore at Mapua in Tasman Bay, between Nelson and Motueka, a few days after Ben and Olivia went missing. Three of them, Peter Beadle, of Greymouth, and Graham Satherley and Bob Melrose, of Mapua, said they spoke to police at the time but were never formally interviewed. The fourth, Mike Kelly of Mapua, wrote to a Waihi man, retired lawyer Peter Keeton, who by early 2000 had begun campaigning to free Scott Watson. 'From the pictures that have been on TV, I and others firmly believe that we have seen that boat,' he wrote to Keeton. 'The ketch was so unusual looking that I did a circuit around it and passed within say 3 metres of it. We saw no signs of life on board.' He said the group contacted the police but they were not interested.

   Pope, still batting off claims that Operation Tam had failed to look under all the necessary stones, described the claims as 'uninformed comment'. He said Operation Tam had received 'many, many hundreds' of ketch sightings. 'For example, a ketch seen in Hawaii on 3 January clearly did not warrant further investigation because it was physically not possible for it to be in [the Marlborough Sounds] at the time. People can make uninformed comment without realising the actual facts or the thrust of the case at the time or how the facts had been revealed.' There was nothing sinister in the fact that the men had not been interviewed by police. 'The fact that ten people may have seen a ketch and hadn't been interviewed may mean that two other witnesses may have seen the same ketch and given a very detailed account of its movements.'

The Ben and Olivia story lasted so long, from their disappearance on New Year's Day 1998 until the Appeal Court hearing in April 2000, that it became a kind of industry. Dozens, maybe hundreds of police, were involved along the way. For some of them, Operation Tam was virtually a full-time job for much of the time. And there were the lawyers, the searchers, the technicians, the forensic scientists, the court staff and the journalists.

Reporters are always on the periphery of any big crime story, but in this case they were at the centre. The reporting of the case itself threatened to become the story at times. There was constant tension between the police's desire to conduct a tidy inquiry and the media's appetite for stories about a case that became enormous almost immediately and stayed that way for months and months.

I often wondered, and was frequently asked, why the story was *so* big. All crimes, let alone all murders, are awful tragedies for the families of the victims. But most of them, most of the time, make a few days' news, if that, before the reporters move on to other stories and leave the victims' families and loved ones to live out their grief privately and anonymously. Most crimes – even killings – rate only a few stories in the papers and seldom a mention on television. The tragedy for the people involved is none the smaller, even if it is arguably easier to deal with if *North & South* and the *New Zealand Women's Weekly* are not knocking on the door asking for exclusives.

From the start, the Ben and Olivia story was never going to be like that. It is hardly a sufficient explanation to point out that, on a mundane level, the disappearance happened during the media's 'silly season' – the dry season for news from Christmas through January – when reporters are desperate for stories to fill the papers and the bulletins. Something more was happening.

Crime as it is depicted in the media usually happens to people who are 'not like us'. Much of the steady stream of crime stories that parades haphazardly and briefly through the newspapers and TV and radio bulletins is about people who were down on their luck long before anything bad enough to be newsworthy happened to them. They were probably poor, they were maybe unemployed, or they came from 'unstable' families. Their fate was unlikely to become a major story, unless there were special circumstances. If the killer or attacker was mentally ill, maybe the crime could highlight shortfalls in mental health services, so it would shift up in the bulletins.

The story of Ben and Olivia fitted none of those circumstances. It demanded attention because it concerned two young people who, as the nation quickly learned on the 6 p.m. TV bulletins, had everything going for them. They were bright, reasonably well-off and attractive. And their awful fate happened in a part of New Zealand that we all thought was untouched and somehow innocent. And it happened at a time of year when everyone was supposed to be having harmless fun. The way it was reported – and the way many people responded to the story – their deaths mattered because they destroyed a myth we like to believe about our country and ourselves: that good, decent people are somehow invulnerable to the random violence and mundane crime that is served up on TV every night. They didn't deserve what happened to them, so Ben and Olivia became something like posthumous celebrities. Their families went to a lot of effort to acknowledge the concern that many New Zealanders expressed about their fate. Yet, after what they have been through, they would be the first to acknowledge that unremarkable and unreported acts of violence and wrong-doing are always tragedies for the people concerned. Nobody deserves what happened to Ben and Olivia.

For a lot of the time while the case was tortuously winding its way through the police and judicial system, I was on a parallel track of my own, slowly putting the book together. From about midway through 1998 the word began to get out that I was writing about the case. At that stage, newspapers were so hungry for fresh 'angles' on the Ben and Olivia story that the writing of a book became something of an intermittent story in itself. Some stories attempted to uncover how the families felt about the book project. Would they co-operate or would they object? I said to reporters that it was my business and the families' business.

Believing it was an angle, the *Sunday News* reported that I still planned to finish the book despite 'taking a high-profile job in Parliament'. 'Wasn't there a conflict of interest?' the reporter wanted to know. The job, with then Prime Minister Jenny Shipley, was very demanding and it did make the task of writing a book seem fairly impossible at times. But mostly it was a mundane difficulty: a matter of finding the time. There were also occasional suggestions from people I talked to that, because I worked in the Prime Minister's office, I somehow had a position on the issues that the case generated. I never quite knew what they meant by that.

Most of all, my involvement with the story brought forward a constant stream of questions and views on the case. Within minutes of meeting anyone, talk would invariably turn to the Ben and Olivia story. People either had a lot of questions or some strongly-held views, often both. Their questions and views followed seasonal changes. Early on, people wanted to know what I thought of the police's conduct of the inquiry; when would Operation Tam ever reach an outcome? When would they finally establish what had happened and arrest someone? Was it true that they were making no progress at all? Alternatively, they wanted to tell me how shoddily the investigation was being handled; they told me about how many obvious leads had been ignored or how the police had made their minds up all along.

Once an arrest had been made, most people wanted to know the 'real' story of what had happened. What were the secrets that police would present in court? Once the case went to trial, first to the depositions in Blenheim and then to the High Court in Wellington, the conversation invariably turned to the gaping holes that people saw in the case as it was being outlined. On the basis of a newspaper story here or there, or a couple of minutes on One Network News, people formed strong conclusions – usually believing that there was no way a conviction could be secured.

After the guilty verdict in the High Court, some of the talk trailed off, but there were still strong opinions. I came across a common feeling that the jury had probably reached the right verdict, but that it had been a bit of a fluke; the evidence hadn't necessarily nailed Scott Watson as conclusively as many would have liked. There was a belief that the verdict was right, but that it was based more on gut instinct than actual evidence. There was interest in the impending appeal, but it was legalistic rather than voyeuristic: the future arguments would hinge on points of law rather than facts.

But throughout it all, people always wanted to know one thing from me: had Scott Watson done it? As if I would know or have access to some special information that the jury hadn't seen.

From early on, I disappointed most people by avoiding any firm opinions of my own, or even engaging in too much conversation. It seemed gratuitous and tasteless to be dining out on a story that, in the end, was not about cops and lawyers and journalists, but about two young people and their families. On another level, it seemed bad luck to be talking about a book that was taking such a long time to write.

And genuinely, I didn't want to be jumping to conclusions of my own; I didn't see my views as very relevant to anyone.

Plenty of other people had views. I had my work cut out keeping track of the opinions and actions that mattered without bothering with opinions of my own.

But in the end I couldn't avoid some opinions of my own. I had spent a lot of time living with the story and inevitably came to some conclusions. I think the investigation was thorough if not flawless. I think the police laboured against impossible odds to put together a strong case. When it came to trial, I was surprised at how laborious and unconstructed much of the Crown's evidence appeared. Given the time the lawyers had been given to prepare, the Crown often seemed to be relying on its sheer bulk of witnesses and evidence rather than a particularly well finessed case. They asked a lot of the jury, and were lucky to get a jury that seemed prepared and able to give a lot. But I was equally surprised at what sometimes appeared to be a desultory case mounted by the defence.

Yet in the end I don't think there was any miscarriage of justice. I think Scott Watson did it, and I think the evidence was strong enough to prove that.

It is, as people say, the small things that can hurt. Mary Smart was at the supermarket one day months after New Year when a stranger made a very odd remark: 'We haven't seen your son for a long time.' 'Sorry?' Mary said, wondering if the woman was trying to be cruel or kind. 'I stared at her for a very long time. Later I realised she meant the sun. We haven't seen the sun for a very long time. She probably thought, That woman's out of her tree.

'Then there are some people who say silly things, like how many children do you have? I say, I've got two girls and my son's missing. They say, Oh yes, I know that. Well, what a stupid bloody question.'

The way they put it, John and Mary Smart long ago settled into a routine of virtually rostering their grief.

Mary: 'We all have down days. John has a down day when I have a good day. We've never had a down day together. I sometimes cry and feel better. Sometimes it's the best thing you can do – to actually grieve and get over it. I wake a lot at night and think about it, but I don't actually get sad in the night. I feel almost peaceful.'

John: 'Sometimes I'm very depressed about it. But you don't show that. We show it to each other, but not to other people.'

'It's nice to grieve,' Mary says. 'It's a privilege to cry and let it all out and then carry on with your life. I just hope it doesn't destroy us as people and make us bitter and angry – and I don't think it will. Because so many people do get like that, and say, Why me, why me?

Mary tried to take some comfort in the fact that she believed she was coping with events as best as she could. She knew her own limits and at least did not have to watch the terrible tragedy happening to someone else, such as a sister or a friend. She reckoned she knew how much she could cope with, but how much could *they* cope with?

'We know people have felt so desperately for us. We've had so much support, and still do. We still have letters put in our letterbox from people saying they're thinking about us. We get flowers about once a month from people we don't know.'

The Smarts do not like 'wearing our grief on our sleeves', as Mary puts it. 'But we do have bad days and nobody else would probably know about that except Jan and Gerald.'

For both families, one of the hardest things to come to grips with is the simple question, Why?

'Coming from where we come from – the families that we both belong to, and the families that Gerald and Jan come from, and the families that 90 percent of New Zealanders come from – we find it really hard to think that somebody out there has had no love in their life. You don't do that. If someone's loved you, or you've loved, you'd never ever, just for no reason, just go and annihilate two people who've had nothing to do with your life.

'But it shows that in his family life there has been a discrepancy of some sort, and for that reason he's to be pitied.'

In different ways, all of the family have tried to keep their grief private. 'I guess we don't like to show each other how much we're hurting,' Mary says. Rebecca Smart lost her brother less than 11 months after her boyfriend's mother was killed in the Raurimu massacre, and she has had counselling which she says has been helpful. Even the Smarts' younger daughter, Annabel, has tried to keep her grief to herself. 'Annabel doesn't cry in front of me because she thinks it's going to hurt me. Whereas I say, It doesn't, we've all got to cry about it. But I think everybody is holding back in front of everyone else. Except John and I don't, do we?'

John lets the question hang. 'We've heard Annabel crying at night upstairs. That really cracks me up. It makes me so angry.'

'It breaks your heart,' says Mary. 'Just sobbing her heart out. I go up and say, Do you want to come down and sleep in our bed? She says, No, I just like being here and thinking about Ben.'